THE STORY OF

NORWOOD

by J. B. Wilson
prepared by H. A. Wilson

The Norwood Society
1990

© London Borough of Lambeth 1973

© The Norwood Society 1990

Reprinted 1990 by Stephen Austin/Hertford

Published by The Norwood Society

Designed by Adrian Hodgkins

ISBN 0 9515384 1 1

Cover picture copied with permission of the former vicar of St. Luke's Church, Rev. J. H. Carroll, by A. C. Inglis for the book "St. Luke, West Norwood 1825–1975".

Copies of the photographs reproduced in this book, together with much other material of local interest, may be consulted, by appointment, at

The Archives Department, Minet Library, 52 Knatchbull Road, London SE5 9QY.

Telephone 071-733 3279

The Norwood Society wishes to acknowledge the donation from J. B. Wilson (Undertaker) Ltd., Norwood High Street, and the assistance received from those members of The Norwood Society who have helped to finance this reprint.

Further Information about The Norwood Society from The Norwood Society, 170 Knights Hill, London SE27 0SR.

Contents

Publisher's Note

The Norwood Society has reprinted The Story of Norwood in its original form despite the fact that the passing of years has resulted in many changes. A few errors have been corrected, however, and where a comment helps the understanding of the script the current situation is noted, but it should be remembered that although first published in 1973, the original manuscript was mostly written before 1949.

Corrigenda

Page 5.	12.	The 1936 rebuilt lodge was destroyed. The crematorium has been found to have been preceded by several others.
	23.	This station has since been rebuilt.
Page 6.	34.	The cinema is now replaced by a DIY store.
	47.	Subsequent research has found this to be incorrect.

Page 9.	line 17(R)	The boroughs are now Lambeth, Croydon, Southwark and Bromley.
Page 13.	line 55(L)	The open water in "Belair" has no linkage with the River Effra and has always been a separate lake.
Page 14.	line 18(L)	The name "Waterloo Churches" is a misnomer as the original plan to commemorate the battle came to nothing.
	line 41(R)	All the bells have now been removed.
Page 15.	line 2(L)	In fact, many of the original roof timbers remain.
Page 18.	line 14(R)	Harriet Waylett's stage name was Kate Kearney.
	line 30(R)	Subsequent research has found that Jeremiah Colman was not buried here.
	line 51(R)	David Cox (Junior).
Page 21.	line 28(R)	The Brotherhood Hall was in Knight's Hill opposite the bus garage.
Page 22.	line 33(R)	Ryecotes. He died in Streatham.
Page 25.	line 48(L)	Now demolished.
Page 26.	line 34(L)	See note for Page 6 no: 34.
Page 27.	line 57(L)	Now demolished, replaced by a block of flats of the same name.
	line 10(R)	See note for Page 18 line 14(R).
	line 48(R)	Disappeared 1952.
Page 28.	line 36(R)	They were both officially called Elder Road.
Page 30.	line 37(L)	Now South London Theatre Centre.
Page 31.	line 18(L)	This is a redevelopment area.
Page 32.	line 37(R)	A redevelopment area.
Page 43.	line 40(L)	Countess of Essex was the actress and singer Kitty Stephens, 1794–1882.
	line 36(R)	This part of Highland Road is now called Vicar's Oak Road.
Page 44.	lines 21–36(L)	This area has been entirely redeveloped and includes a new Salvation Army Hall, supermarket, community centre, shops and garden centre.
Page 44.	line 5(R)	Closed 1990.
	line 14(R)	Acquired by the Greek community in 1977 and is now the Greek Orthodox Church of St. Constantine and St. Helen.
	line 44(R)	Now "The Sportsman".
	line 47(R)	Now demolished.
Page 46.	line 4(L)	The Lawns was a mansion built after the decline of Beulah Spa and demolished in the 1960's after a fire. Tivoli Lodge is all that remains of the original Spa buildings.
Page 47.		The following have been demolished: All Saints' Schoolhouse, Grangemount, Roselawn, Westwood, Little Menlo (1960) and The Priory.
	line 33(R)	Colonel Gouraud.
Page 50.	line 4(R)	The firm was called Maudslay, Sons and Field.
Page 52.	line 51(L)	Demolished 1990.
	line 49(R)	Demolished 1990.
Page 53.	line 6(L)	The railway contractor was John Tredwell of Leigham Court, Streatham.
Page 54.	lines 46–49(L)	Chapel, cottages, shops and The Rosemary Branch all demolished when the bus garage was enlarged.
Page 55.	line 24(L)	See note for page 5 no: 23.
	line 47(L)	Signal box closed and demolished.
Page 56.	line 25(L)	Now replaced by a petrol station.
	line 53(R)	See page 6 no: 26.
Page 57.	line 1(L)	Lord James Hannen.
Page 62.	line 48(L)	All Saints' Church is Norwood's only Grade I listed building.
	line 53(R)	Has now been rebuilt.
Page 64.	line 14(R)	All that remains is the tower: the rest was burned down and rebuilt in the 1980's.
	line 48(R)	Wesleyan church and cottages demolished; rebuilt as smaller church and superstore.
Page 65.	line 15(L)	The Woodman has been demolished.
	line 32(L)	See note page 44 line 47(R).

List of illustrations

overhead wire system, before conversion to the third conductor rail (1928).

25. Original horse-bus and tram terminus in Norwood Road opposite the Thurlow Arms.

26. Original gateway to St. Luke's Church and entrance to Norwood Cemetery. The building bearing the name "Yeatman" was later used by the Civil Defence and is now part of the site of West Norwood Library and Nettlefold Hall. The fountain was presented by Mrs. Woodford Fawcett, a prominent Temperance worker. On the left, the end of the tram-lines, at that time the terminus.

27. One of the old trams that used to run from the top of Anerley Hill to West Croydon.

28. London House, premises of J. B. Wilson (Undertaker) Ltd., 103, Norwood High Street, about 1870.

29. Milk deliverymen from Bacon's Dairy.

30. Outside the Thurlow Arms (note coat of arms above door), Mrs. Williams's greengrocery stall.

31. An old shop which stood in Chapel Road on the corner of Jaffray Place. Mr. Naph Harris also had a business near the Elephant & Castle.

32. John Peed's nursery and market garden in Norwood Road, at the junction of Leigham Vale and Palace Road.

33. Greengrocer's shop in Norwood High Street on the corner of Windsor Road (now Grove) formerly owned by the Thewless family. Later it became Kingston's of Herne Hill.

34. Norwood Broadway, built 1888–1890. The outward appearance is similar today—some shops still have canopies; cannon-ball decoration at the apex of the roof sections is mostly intact, likewise the turret on the right of the picture (though without its pointed roof). Even the plate bearing the name "The Broadway" remains, above the shop on the corner of Lancaster Avenue. The tree on the left stands in the garden of the site now occupied by the Top Rank Bingo Hall (formerly the Regal Cinema).

35. The Horns Tavern, Knight's Hill (note the older building behind being demolished), adjacent to the site of the original "Horns" shown on Rocque's map of 1745. Note also the granite blocks in the roadway, believed to be under the present road and the fire-alarm in the centre.

36. A former building of the King's Head in Norwood High Street. The entrance on the right led to gardens at the rear where open-air theatricals used to be given, known as the Tivoli Gardens.

37. View from Norwood Park showing what are now known as Elderwood and Inglewood Old People's Homes. These together with Wood Vale (now demolished) occupied the site of the Lambeth House of Industry for the Infant Poor (1810) the first Poor Law school in the country. Also in the picture is the cottage (illus. no. 18) retained as a park-keeper's cottage, demolished by fire in 1942.

38. Norwood Technical College showing the enclosed wooden staircase built as an emergency fire-escape on instructions from the London County Council.

39. St. Luke's Church School on the corner of Elder Road and Linton Grove. Built in 1825 and added to in 1850. This photograph was taken after a fire, all the children having been safely evacuated. The front wall of the building collapsed in 1901.

40. The well-house of Beulah Spa, Beulah Hill in 1830.

41. Lord George Sanger's circus which used to visit Norwood annually on the waste ground which used to lie between St. Louis, St. Gothard and St. Cloud Roads.

42. Some of the West Norwood Cycle Club who used to meet at the Bricklayers' Arms in Chapel Road.

43. Crystal Palace Football Club, 1908–9.

44. Cottage in Knight's Hill near Ernest Avenue, which was converted into Lower (West) Norwood's first police station.

45. West Norwood Fire Station when it was situated in Norwood High Street. The building later became St. Luke's parish hall and then the premises of the South London Theatre Club.

46. Flooding in Wood Street (now Dunbar Place) after a bad thunderstorm on 14th June, 1914. The River Effra, which flows under the street, is now enclosed as a sewer.

47. The first-ever aeroplane flight in Great Britain. One of the Wright brothers flying from the old cycle track and sports ground at Crystal Palace.

48. Reflections from the Crystal Palace fire, 1936, seen from Westow Hill. Note the fire engine jammed in by traffic. Photograph by J. B. Wilson.

Foreword

In presenting "The Story of Norwood" to the reader, it is obviously essential to begin with a word of explanation, as it will soon become apparent that much of what is contained herein is already past history, although written in the present tense. Buildings have been demolished, bombed sites have been cleared and many new buildings erected; war damaged churches have been demolished and some completely new churches have risen from the dust and ashes. Vicars and Ministers have come and gone. The reader might well be tempted to ask, "Why these discrepancies?"—hence this word of explanation.

My brother, the late James Benson Wilson, was a great lover of Norwood and its history and he collected many old prints of the district and carefully studied its history, making extensive researches to ascertain true facts and sparing no pains to make sure of the accuracy of his story. His unexpected death at the early age of 44 in December, 1949, left a big gap. Unfortunately, a man's memory dies with him. Much useful information and, most important of all, many sources of such information, were therefore lost to those who would complete the work on which he had started.

At the time of his death we were still troubled with paper restrictions, and publications of a purely local and personal nature were difficult to put into circulation. In the midst of a very busy life, however, I have always had at the back of my mind that when an opportune occasion arose, I would like to see the book in print as a memorial to my brother's devotion to the district and a memento of his untiring efforts to make this a story known to many.

At last, with the aid of several kind friends, including the late Mr. A. W. Maby, who helped with the index, and Mr. W. F. Broome, the Principal Assistant Librarian, Lambeth, I have been able to reach this satisfactory position. What then was I to do? Was I to revise the whole of the script? This would mean so many alterations that the story could hardly be described as my brother's.

Finally, I have decided to let the book go forward in the original form he left it in December, 1949, for, after all, a history has to stop somewhere at its point of publication; so here then we have "The Story of Norwood" up to 1950. Perhaps at some future time, some other historian, filled with a similar love of the district, may decide to take up pen and continue the story.

I might add that it is in this form that the manuscript was copied and is now kept in the Greater London Council's historical archives, a further point which decided me to leave the story in its original state.

Some may question and say, "Who is this man?" Or to quote the words of Scripture, "By what authority doeth he this?" In Chapter 6, dealing with the Norwood High Street, you will see that the Wilson family moved to this district in 1830 and the family have been actively connected with the locality ever since that time. We are therefore definitely the oldest family of direct descent in the district and certainly the oldest in conducting business with the public. The late vicar of St. Luke's, Dr. F. J. Lambert, once asked me how it was that my brother was able to collect so much information and so many old photographs of the area. The answer is that in the course of his business he was always coming into contact with elderly people and had access to their homes. This has gone on for five generations, and much knowledge of the district has been passed down from father to son.

HARRY A. WILSON

THE GREAT NORTH WOOD.

Norwood, and its surrounding neighbourhood, as Surveyed by Rocque in 1745.

Chapter I
Earliest Days

Happy is the town that has no history. If that is true then Norwood must be a happy place, for the story of Norwood contains no spectacular history. There are no castles to speak of, no great battles to recall, neither is there any truth in the rumour that Queen Elizabeth once sailed up the River Effra in a steamboat as far as Dulwich. This is only a simple story describing the growth of the district from a mere hamlet to a suburb of Greater London, but it is a story which has a great fascination for those who have spent most of their lives in Norwood.

How did the district get its name? I think it is well known that the name came from the North Wood. To this wood we owe the fact that Norwood has no history, for little more than a hundred years ago the whole of this district was thickly covered with the trees of this wood. Why, you may ask, was it called the North Wood when it was to the south of London? The answer is that this district was part of the county of Surrey and the wood covered most of the north part of that county, stretching from Croydon almost to Camberwell. The earliest certain record of it appears to have been made in the Assize Rolls of 1272. In the reign of Edward III (1327–77) it came into the possession of the Whitehorse family. A Walter Whitehorse was the King's shield-bearer in 1368.

Norwood figures in a work of fiction entitled *The Journal of the Plague Year* written by Daniel Defoe, the author of "Robinson Crusoe," in 1722. This is the actual quotation from that book:—

"And as I have been told that several that wandered into the country on the Surrey side were found starved to death in the woods and commons, that country being more open and more woody than any other part so near London, especially about Norwood, the parishes of Camberwell, Dullege and Luseme (Lewisham) where it seems no body durst relieve the poor distressed people for fear of infection."

Another early mention of Norwood was by Aubrey in the second volume of his "Perambulation of Surrey", wherein he speaks of "A great wood belonging to the Archbishops." It is said to have consisted wholly of oaks, and among them was one that bore mistletoe. It is also recorded that the wood was seized from the Archbishops of Canterbury by Oliver Cromwell, and at this time consisted of 830 acres—"But such havoc had been committed in it that it contained only 9,200 oaken pollards and eighty timber trees."

There was in the wood an immense tree of great age called the "Vicar's Oak." At the spot where the tree stood no less than four parishes met—Lambeth, Camberwell, Croydon, and Battersea—and at the periodical Beating of the Bounds ceremony the various parochial authorities used to meet there, a fact recorded in old Parish accounts. I will quote a few examples from the Lambeth Churchwardens' Accounts, as printed by the Surrey Record Society:

1583—"When we went our perambulation at viccars oke in rogation weke 2/6d
For a drinkinge the same daye 6d
1585—"For makinge honest men drinke when we went to vicars oke in perambulacion 2/6d
1597—"At the Aleynges heade when we went out arambelacyon to vickers oke .... 6/od."

Evidently the ceremony gained in popularity as the years went by. In 1635 "at the parambulacion goeinge to vicars Oake" the amount had reached £3 8s. 6d. Were the Vicar's Oak standing today it would be in front of the White Swan Hotel by the roundabout at the top of Anerley Hill on the Palace Parade. This spot is still the boundary of the boroughs of Lambeth, Croydon, Camberwell and urban district of Penge, once a detached portion of Battersea. Badrices Eye, as Battersea was called, once stood as an island struggling against the encroaching waters of the Thames. In a charter of as long ago as A.D. 957 dealing with "Batricesee" is the wood called Penge. Battersea, being mostly low-lying, lacked wood for fuel and house-building, and the connection with this usefully wooded portion of the parish continued till 1888. The Vicar's Oak is shown on a map made in 1808, and Allen in his *History of Lambeth* (1825) describing the boundaries of the district of St. Luke, says:—

"... to corner of Hall Green." [By the present Paxton Hotel] "thence it makes an obtuse angle SE, and proceeds along an old hedge-row, crossing the parish highway leading to Dulwich, to a LP [Lambeth Parish] post on the SE side thereof, thence following the hedge on the east side of Beaulieu-road, to a LP post at the spot from whence the road diverges from the said hedge, and continuing along an old hedge, and passing several parish posts up to the Vicar's Oak; thence it makes an acute angle, and passes along the North side of Vicar's Oak Road [Westow Hill] all the way to the corner of Elder-road where it crosses Vicar's Oak-road ... and where there are several parish marks; and thence, making a square angle, it passes along the South side of the Vicar's Oak-road [Crown Dale] and Streatham-lane [Crown Lane] to the corner of Streatham-common."

So the Vicar's Oak was still standing in 1825 on the very summit of the hill 379 feet above sea level.

The North Wood, being largely composed of oak trees, rapidly disappeared under the axes of the woodmen who lived in their little huts in the wood. A picture of one of these woodmen, with his dog at his heels and a bundle of faggots over his shoulder, was painted on the signboard of "The Woodman" public house at Upper Norwood. There was a great amount of charcoal-burning too: it was one of the chief trades of Croydon, and is perpetuated in the name of a road—Collier's Water Lane, Thornton Heath. How rapidly the wood disappeared can be seen on a map published in 1746. It was a map of

London and its environs by John Rocque, and shows that the wood was then only about 3 miles wide at its widest part. As the trees were cut down the waste land which remained was marked as common, and on Rocque's map we find Croydon Common, Penge Common, Streatham Common, Knight's Hill Common, Dulwich Common, and Westwood Common. It is a very interesting map, and shows many roads or tracks which were in existence through the North Wood. As the map is marked with all the contours of the ground a fair idea of the course of these tracks is given. Knight's Hill and Knight's Hill Common are shown as being on the site of the present road called Knight's Hill, West Norwood, with the "Horns Tavern" near the foot of it, and Knight's Hill Pound at the top of it near the corner of the present Crown Lane. On the map can be seen "Crocksted Lane", Dulwich College, and also the Dulwich Wells and the Sydenham Wells. The district of Herne Hill is marked as "Island Green".

There can be little doubt that the real development of the district began with the Croydon Enclosure Act of 1797. Briefly, this was an act appointing Enclosure Commissioners, and laying down the procedure for enclosing the lands. There were enclosure acts before this date but the act of 1797 was the biggest and most important one. The Rev. D. W. Garrow's "History of Croydon" published in 1818 gives the following account of this act:—

"In the year 1797, an Act of Parliament was obtained for the purpose of enclosing the waste lands of Norwood, which were made freehold, and the Archbishop, Dr. Moore granted a building lease of the land belonging to the See. Since that period, the number of dwelling-houses has increased to about 150; and the number of inhabitants must be near 1000."

And later in the same book:—

"In the year 1797, an Act of Parliament was obtained, by which it was provided that if the Commissioners should find that the inhabitants of Croydon had any right of common on Norwood, or in the woods there, they should set out as an equivalent for such right, 215 acres in some of the commons of Croydon, which should be vested in the vicar, churchwardens, and overseers for the time being, . . . The power of the trustees having been established as to the investment, they applied to Parliament in 1806 for an Act to enable them to sell these lands."

There were several subsequent enclosure acts affecting Norwood. One was in 1806, and was called the Rush Common Act (46 Geo. 3 c.lvii) from which we learn that there were within the Manor of Lambeth in the County of Surrey certain common lands containing 200 acres and upwards and that the Archbishop of Canterbury, in the right of his archi-episcopal see, was lord of the manor, and was seized of divers woods and wood grounds in the said manor. Also that Edward, Lord Thurlow, William Cole, and divers other persons as owners of tenements, claimed rights of common pasture over the woods and of taking certain wood therefrom for firewood, and that the common lands if divided and enclosed might be greatly improved. How the lands were divided is shown on two plans made under the Enclosure Act.

The plan relating to the Croydon part of the district is dated 1800, and to the Lambeth part 1808. The plans clearly show each plot of land with the owner or owners thereof: on both plans many plots are marked "His Grace the Archbishop of Canterbury," and on the Norwood section of the Lambeth plan many are marked "Rt. Hon. Lord Thurlow". Many plots are marked with the letter "C" which, says a footnote to the plan, means "copyhold." Mr. F. R. Stead in his book *Title Deeds Old and New* (page 6) speaking of Copyhold says:—

". . . by the time of Bracton, a famous Judge in the reign of Henry III, the Lords had begun to keep customary Court Rolls, on which the names of tenants were entered . . . the copy of the Court Roll came to be regarded as the tenant's title to his holding."

Hence the word "Copyhold". All Copyholds were turned into Freeholds on the 1st January, 1926.

It is interesting to compare these Enclosure Act plans with Rocque's map made 60 years earlier. It can be seen that the North Wood had disappeared by 1800 all but a few large coppices, and the roads of Norwood as we know them today were beginning to take shape. On the Croydon section of the map, Beulah Hill, Gibsons Hill, Biggin Hill, Spa Hill, South Norwood Hill, Whitehorse Lane and Green Lane are shown. On the Norwood section of the plan, Norwood Road, Knight's Hill, Norwood High Street, Elder Road, Chapel Road, Gipsy Road, Benton's Lane, Crown Dale, Salter's Hill, Central Hill, Gipsy Hill and Westow Hill are shown, so these are the oldest roads in the district. These names are those by which these roads are known today. I will refer to their earlier names as I come to them.

Strangely enough, neither of these two plans show Norwood's river, the Effra, and Rocque's map only shows a small portion of it marked with the name "The Shore". It is however shown on another very interesting map drawn in 1825, and used as a frontispiece for Allen's "History of Lambeth". This map shows little alteration from the enclosure map of 1808 as far as the roads are concerned, but it does show that quite a number of houses and other buildings had been erected in the twenty years that had passed. A turnpike gate is marked across the Norwood Road at a point just below the junction of Knight's Hill and Norwood High Street near the present tram terminus. The original plan of Norwood Cemetery shows this road as a "Turnpike Road to Sydenham". The boundaries of St. Luke's parish are marked on Allen's map. The parish stretched from Upper Tulse Hill and Trinity Rise in the North to Crown Dale and Central Hill in the South, and from Leigham Court Road in the West to Gipsy Hill in the East. This area has since been divided into several parishes.

I have already referred to the boundary of the parish as set out in Allen's book. The boundary was marked by many posts, marks, and stones. The Lambeth parish boundary mark took the form of a letter L superimposed on a letter P. One of these marks can still be seen as a tablet let into the brick wall which runs at the top of Perran Road from Mr.

Keywood's, the upholsterer's, to the corner of Christchurch Road. Some more boundary marks can be seen at the spot where Streatham Common begins in Crown Lane.

With the passing of the North Wood came the division of the land into districts. Norwood was divided into South, Upper, and Lower Norwood, the last being the original "village" situated in a hollow almost surrounded by hills. It was only natural therefore that it should be called "Lower Norwood". So it remained for many years but about 1880 there was a great agitation to change this name. Was Lower Norwood considered *infra dig*, I wonder?

Did it imply that it was the abode of a lower class of people? I cannot say, but there was an objection to the name. But there were also objections to changing the name too. Those connected with the Lower Norwood Building Society foresaw considerable difficulties in respect to title deeds of properties, etc. Then of course there was the Post Office to be considered and the Brighton Railway Company to convince. However, the change came about eventually, chiefly through the perseverance of Mr. Truslove of the *Norwood Press*, said Mr. H. J. Bromley, the auctioneer and estate agent, and in 1885, Lower Norwood became West Norwood.

Chapter 2
The River Effra

Old Norwood people are apt to speak of Norwood's river, the Effra, as though the River Thames is a mere trickle in comparison. But in actual fact, at the Norwood end of Lambeth, the Effra was just a small stream running between very muddy banks, and was by no means a thing of beauty. The English Place-name Society's volume on Surrey (page 3) gives Brayley (1840) as the earliest instance of the name Effra being used for the stream. It indicates the rather vague possibility that Effra may represent the Old English "Heah efre" or high bank. At various times when rainfall was exceptionally heavy it refused to remain a stream, and really lived up to its title River, and often caused severe flooding. One of the worst of these floods occurred in the summer of 1890, and let into the wall on the south side of the old relieving office at the end of Elder Road can be seen a white stone tablet bearing this inscription:—

FLOOD LEVEL
17th July 1890

the line marking the height of the flood waters which on that occasion swept away the brick boundary wall of the convent at the foot of Crown Dale, flooding all the low-lying parts of West Norwood. Another of these bad floods occurred on Sunday, 14th June, 1914. A terrific thunderstorm broke about mid-day and for nearly three hours there was almost continuous thunder and lightning (which struck several places in West Norwood) accompanied by torrential rain and huge hailstones. This caused the River Effra to overflow from the brick sewer in which it had been enclosed for many years, and once again all the low-lying parts of Norwood were under water to a considerable depth. In Ernest Street, East Place, Auckland Place, Wood Street, Dunbar Street, Robson Road and Chestnut Road the ground floors of the houses were all flooded, and in some cases Sunday joints were washed out of ovens. Many people were rendered temporarily homeless, and the Public Hall on Knight's Hill was opened that night to make sleeping quarters for them. The Vicar of St. Luke's and the West Norwood Brotherhood organised a relief fund to help the victims.

The same thing happened twice in the 1920's, and on one of these occasions I remember several young men were awarded medals for rescuing animals trapped by the floods in East Place. In 1935, however, steps were taken to stop this flooding, and the Effra sewer was enlarged. Deep shafts were sunk at the lower end of Norwood High Street, in Chestnut Road, and in Rosendale Road. This job took many months. I have set its misdeeds before you first in order to show that our river was a mixed blessing. In fact it was a good thing for Norwood when this treasure was laid up in earth, so to speak, where

weeds do not corrupt nor midges sting as they do where the River Wandle still runs in the open around Norbury and Mitcham. Although the Wandle runs in a concrete bed it tends to get slimy, and to breed flies by the thousand, to say nothing of smells.

Let us now follow the course of the River Effra from source to mouth with all the little tributaries which fed it. There were two main branches of the River Effra at the Norwood end of Lambeth. The larger branch had its source on the slope between Church Road, Upper Norwood and Harold Road. The little pond in the recreation ground by the Harold Road end of Chevening Road was connected with the head waters of it. The stream flowed behind the north side of Chevening Road and across the dip in Hermitage Road. There was a little bridge over the stream at the back of the present Newtown, though bridge is hardly the word, for it consisted of four planks across the wide ditch. After crossing Hermitage Road, it ran through the grounds of the convent where, at a point opposite Elder Road, it took a right-hand turn thus changing its course from a westerly to a northerly direction. Crossing the present Crown Dale at its lowest point it swung round through that cultivated piece of ground at the corner of Crown Dale and Elder Road, almost immediately crossing Elder Road to the east side, flowing through the present Norwood Park in front of the little thatched cottages that used to stand there. The occupants of these cottages crossed the stream by little wooden bridges to get to the road. From Norwood Park it flowed through the fields, across what is now the lowest part of Norwood Park and Eylewood Roads. When it was placed underground there were two iron gratings in the fields here, and small boys would drop paper boats down one of these gratings into the water below, then run like mad to the other grating to see them sail by. The stream then went on to cross Gipsy Road, passing through the present school playground, along the bottom end of Windsor Grove following the west side of the railway embankment. Here it formed itself into two large ponds known locally as "The Reservoir". Thence along East Place to the railway arch where this turning joins Pilgrim Hill behind the "Hope" public house.

Here it was joined by a tributary which had its source at the top end of Casewick Road by the corner of Cheviot and Greenhurst Roads, flowing down between the back gardens of Cheviot and Casewick Roads. A portion of the bed of this stream can still be seen at the back of the tennis courts at the bottom of Cheviot Road. This stream caused quite a bit of bother with the foundations at the back of the Brotherhood Hall when it was built on Knight's Hill. From the back of the Brotherhood buildings the tributary crossed the bottom of Thornlaw Road and Knight's Hill into Knight's Hill Square (where it was itself joined by another little tributary having its source at the back of Jaffray Place, and which flowed across Rothschild Street and the lowest part of Ernest Avenue into Knight's Hill Square). From there it proceeded across Langmead Square and High Street by the side of the "Hope" public house, where it joined the main stream.

Here the Effra turned at a right angle across Auckland Hill and Auckland Place to the bottom of Dunbar Place, turning left along the cemetery wall at the back of this turning and across the bottom end of Dunbar Street where it passed under Norwood Cemetery. After passing under the cemetery it crossed Robson Road, at a point where there is a gap in the houses and on to Chestnut Road. Here it turned right, and passed along Chestnut Road itself for a few yards before turning half-left again to the corner of Idmiston and Ardlui Roads, thence to the corner of Hexham and Towton Roads. After crossing Lavengro, Tulsemere and Dalmore Roads it passed across the crossroads of Rosendale and Thurlow Park Roads, and on the north side of this road, almost opposite where Carson Road runs into Thurlow Park Road, it was joined by the second main branch which we will now trace from its source to this point.

The second branch of the Effra had its source on the north side of Westow Hill, flowing down the back of Woodland Road, crossing the end of Colby Road to a point where Gipsy Hill meets The Avenue. It then proceeded down the field at the foot of Gipsy Hill, crossing Gipsy Road by the Paxton Hotel, round the back of the Paxton Yard and Surrey Mews to a point by the "Crown" in Hamilton Road. (Here it was joined by a small tributary which had its source between Alexandra Drive and Bristow Road.) It crossed Bristow Road, Sainsbury Road and under the railway to the point where Oaks Avenue joins Gipsy Road. Then crossing this road behind the "Two Towers" it flowed behind the right-hand side of that part of Rommany Road opposite Salters Hill School to the "Crown" in Hamilton Road. From this point the stream continued between Clive and South Croxted Roads along the back of Chalford Road, passing right along the back of Clive Road, and crossed Park Hall Road, along the bottom of Elmworth Grove, and the back of Carson Road. Then it crossed Thurlow Park Road, and joined up with the other branch.

Following the line of Thurlow Park Road the Effra then passed across Croxted Road, and then after passing under the railway it turned sharp left to pass through the grounds of "Belair" where there is still some open water. It then proceeded across Turney Road, following the line of Burbage Road to Half Moon Lane, along which it turned and flowed to the railway bridge at Herne Hill. Here it was joined by another fairly large tributary, the course of which we will now follow.

This tributary started at the top of Leigham Vale, and flowed right down the railway side of this road to the railway bridge at Tulse Hill. Here, having joined with a small streamlet from Penrith Place, it turned down the Norwood Road itself from John Peed's Nursery to the corner of Perran Road where it was again joined by a small stream which flowed down between Christchurch Road and Tulse Hill. From Perran Road it crossed to the Dulwich side of Norwood Road, proceeding along this side of Norwood Road until at a point opposite Deronda Road it crossed over to the foot of Trinity Rise. From there it flowed along the line of Norwood Road inside Brockwell Park railings, once again crossing to the Dulwich side of Norwood Road before it linked up with the River Effra by the railway bridge at Herne Hill.

Here strictly speaking the River Effra has passed out of the Norwood district, but I think it will be interesting to follow its course the whole way. From Herne Hill it flowed along Dulwich Road to Effra Parade where another tributary joined it.

This tributary had its source by the ponds in Brockwell Park, and flowed down the park side of Tulse Hill to a point in Water Lane behind the "George Canning". Close by this it was joined by another stream flowing from Upper Tulse Hill (behind Leander Road) which crossed the bottom of Tulse Hill. The main tributary turned right along Water Lane to meet the Effra at Effra Parade.

From Dulwich Road corner the Effra flowed along the Brixton Hill side of Dalberg Road, and crossed Mervan, Kellett and Saltoun Roads to the crossroads of Coldharbour Lane and Atlantic Road. Then it curved under the railways and crossed Popes Road to Brixton Road by the police station. It flowed right down the Camberwell side of Brixton Road, and from there almost to Kennington Church, being joined on the way by a small tributary at the corner of Angell Road. At Kennington Church the river turned left, and, passing round Kennington Oval, turned away to Vauxhall Park. Then after turning right a short distance along the line of South Lambeth Road it turned left across this road, under the railway lines and into the River Thames at a point between Nine Elms Lane and Vauxhall Bridge.

Alfred S. Foord's book, *Springs, Streams and Spas of London* published in 1910, says:

> "To speak of the River Effra as a River was an extravagance for in point of fact the 'River' partook more of the character of a moderately capacious stream . . .",

though later Foord says, speaking of the Brixton Road portion of the river,

> "Here it became larger, its average size along the main road was about 12 feet wide and 6 feet deep."

Thus flowed, and sometimes overflowed, the River Effra, its name perpetuated in Effra Road, Effra Parade, and Water Lane. Although it has been out of sight since before I was born, yet I have seen its water flowing along, for a bomb which fell at the corner of Angell Road and Brixton Road during the "Blitz" uncoverd its brick sewer.

Chapter 3
St. Luke's Church

We have seen that development of West Norwood began at the time of the Enclosure Act of 1808. In those days the church of St. Mary, Lambeth, was the parish church for this district. As a matter of interest I have still the "marriage lines" of my great-great-grandfather which read thus:—

> "St. Mary, Lambeth, Surrey.
> James Benson Wilson, batchelor, and Ann Edwards, Spinster, both of this Parish, were Married in this Church by Banns the third day of June 1814 as appears by the Register Book of Marriages belonging to the Parish of Lambeth from whence the above is extracted, By me, J. T. Barrett, curate."

It was in the latter part of 1822 that work was begun on four churches in Lambeth—St. Matthew's, Brixton; St. Mark's, Kennington; St. Luke's, West Norwood; and St. John's, Waterloo Road. The four churches were known as "Waterloo" churches, also as "Half-price" churches. The reason was that the money for the building came in a special way. Half of the money for each church was found in the district in which the church was built, and the other half came from money presented by the Government to the Church of England in commemoration of the peace which followed the Battle of Waterloo. St. Matthew's, St. Mark's and St. John's were all completed and opened in the year 1824, but St. Luke's was not completed until the following year owing to the fact that there was a great deal of controversy concerning the lay-out of the interior. St. Luke's and St. John's were both designed by Mr. Bedford of Camberwell, and were almost exactly alike except for the towers. The tower of St. Luke's is an almost exact copy of the tower of Holy Trinity, Newington, of which Mr. Bedford was also architect.

The architect's estimate for the church of St. Luke was £12,387 8s. 3d. including incidental expenses and commissions, and the first contract was £11,457 13s. 6d., but it almost goes without saying that the estimate was not enough, and by the time the church was completed nearly £18,000 had been spent. The style of the church is Grecian, with tower and portico, and it had many peculiar features. Allen's *History of Lambeth* published in the year (1825) that the church was completed gives a good description of it on pages 430-434, which, epitomised, reads:-

> "This Church is in part of the Parish (Lambeth) completely detached from the populous suburbs of the Great Metropolis and in spite of buildings fast arising will still be in the country.
> "Therefore, Grecian Church is more out of character here than in Brixton. Surely a pointed spire of Old English Style would have far better assimilated with the adjoining verdant scenery than the present octagon which from a distance gives idea of anything rather than a Church Tower. A Pepper-box elevated into a steeple can have no charms, rather regarded as an unsightly object, more so by the unappropriate situation which has been chosen for it. There are galleries and organ at West End and no others. The Altar is against the East (High Street) wall. Extra gallery across East and central window converted into a door. Pulpit and reading desk in similar part of opposite wall. Everything therefore out of proper place and interior injured by these alterations. Commandments merely inscribed on Tablets of marble fixed to wall above Altar. The organ is at present merely temporary, it is an old instrument. Church plate presented by the Archbishop of Canterbury."

Evidently Mr. Allen did not think much of our parish church when it was first built. The "alterations" he speaks of are obviously those that held up the building. Certainly it must have looked unorthodox to say the least, to enter the main door of the church to find the altar halfway down on the left-hand wall and the pulpit on the opposite side. The pulpit was a "three decker", and the sexton had his desk immediately under it. As clerk, a good deal of responsibility fell to the sexton on Sundays, including the control of the women pew-openers and the beadle. For many years the sexton was Mr. John Thorn whose grandson was also verger at a later date. The gallery at the end by the organ was occupied by the children from the Lambeth Schools in Elder Road. St. Luke's Church was dedicated on the 15th July, 1825 by Dr. Manners Sutton, the then Archbishop of Canterbury. It was he who presented the handsome set of communion plate still in use. It was not until 1836 that the district was separated from the parish of Lambeth and so became an independent parish. In later years the parish was of course again split up into other independent parishes.

The clock in the tower, put there in 1826, was made by Vulliamy of London. This clock was renovated in the 1920's by Messrs. Gillette & Johnson of Croydon, and the old black face which was so difficult to see was replaced by a white face which is illuminated at night. The cost of this work was raised by public subscription. The tubular bells were replaced in the tower in 1892. Two bells had been put in the tower when the church was built, the clock striking on a large bell while the smaller bell called the parishioners to the service. In the year 1943 an apparatus was installed to broadcast recordings of church bells from the tower.

The church seats nearly 1,000 people in the nave, and one-fifth of these seats must by Act of Parliament be kept free. Under the church is an extensive crypt in which were the coffins of several departed parishioners. These coffins were all bricked in during the war of 1914–1918 when the crypt was used, as it was in the more recent war, as an air-raid shelter. Important alterations and improvements to the church were made between 1852 and 1854, but the most important were made in the year 1870 when the roof was found to be in such a bad state of repair that an entirely new roof had to be built. On May 12th of that year the vestry meeting appointed a committee to make arrangements for the necessary work, and a fund was opened for the restoration which cost £6,000, of which a Mr. Quilter and Mr. H. H. Leaf contributed more than £1,000 between them. Mr. G. E. Street was the architect employed for this work, and the interior was completely redesigned on his plan. In addition to the new roof, the old galleries were done away with, and the altar was put in the more orthodox place facing the main doors. The main reredos was a very beautiful one of carved alabaster showing a cross, in the centre of which stood the Lamb of God. This reredos was removed when the church was redecorated in 1936, and was replaced by an altar with a carved oak canopy of much more modern design. There were nine stained-glass windows in the church (many of them now destroyed by bomb-blast) seven of them illustrating scenes in the life of Our Lord. One pictures the story of the Good Samaritan, and the one above the altar shows the Four Evangelists with Our Lord in their midst. The scene of Mary Magdalene in the garden is the only remaining window, now in the lady chapel. In 1934 new choir stalls were erected, and a magnificent carved oak screen which extends the whole width of the church. The screen came from the church of St. Sepulchre, Holborn and was given by the late Mr. Thomas Knowlden. Another heavily-carved screen is the Portal screen in front of the Lady Chapel. The erection of the former screen made the position of the font, just to the left of the main door, very inconvenient as it restricted the space around it, so in 1943 the font was moved to its present position inside the screen near the east wall. On the wall near the original site of the font is a marble tablet which was an original altar slab of the church. In addition to recording the details of the dedication of the church it also gives the list of vicars of St. Luke's as follows:—

George d'Oyley, D.D., Rector of Lambeth
Arthur Gibson, Licensed Curate
1836 Charles Turner
1857 John W. Lester, D.D.
1870 Leveson C. Randolph
1876 John Gilmore
1891 Henry W. Cooper
1900 Herbert T. Hughes
1911 W. Goldsborough Whittam
1921 Francis Sardeson
1925 W. Heaton Heaton-Renshaw
1931 Norman Hook, M.A.
1936 S. Wilson Ruscoe
1943 C. R. Farnsworth, M.A.

Of the first vicars I have no record except for a mention of Dr. Lester in the log book of St. Luke's Day School. The Rev. John Gilmore went to a living at St. Lawrence, near Ramsgate. The Rev. Henry W. Cooper, M.A., was a very able man whose views were considered somewhat High Church at that time,

and he quickly filled the church. The Rev. H. T. Hughes came from the colonies. The Rev. W. Goldsborough Whittam was a most lovable man, liked wherever he went. Then after the Rev. Francis Sardeson came the energetic Rev. W. H. Heaton-Renshaw who will be remembered for the splendid alterations which were made to the parish hall during his time. The Rev. Norman Hook who succeeded him was a fine tall scholarly man, a very thoughtful and earnest preacher who did good work in Norwood. Then came the much-loved Rev. S. Wilson Ruscoe from Saltwood. The news of his death came as a great shock to Norwood, and his passing was a great loss to the parish. A beautiful cross has been placed in the church, together with a marble tablet by the main door, recording that the cross was placed there to his honoured memory. He was succeeded by the Rev. C. R. Farnsworth who came from Ramsgate, and is now at Newport, Isle of Wight.

The parish has been fortunate in having so many splendid vicars, and fortunate also in the many fine men who have been curates at the church. The Rev. H. W. Cooper had as his curate the Rev. H. Stansfield Prior, M.A., one of the most popular of St. Luke's curates. He married Miss Hester Vaughan Sloman, daughter of Dr. Sloman, the organist of St. Luke's. She was a brilliant musician, one of the best pianoforte players Norwood has known. Among other well-remembered curates were: the Rev. A. G. P. Baines, a good footballer who played for West Norwood; tbe Rev. W. E. Clemens, chaplain to the Lambeth Schools and Norwood Cemetery; the Rev. F. M. Anderson; the Rev. H. Loy; Rev. M. Brice; the Rev. E. C. Cook; the Rev. D. Harbord, and the Rev. R. S. G. Bradshaw.

In addition to Dr. Sloman, Mr. Carey, Mr. Percy C. Bright, F.R.C.O. (who died in 1945) and Mr. Henry Hall, who was killed with his wife and daughter in an air raid in 1940, were all well-known organists and choir masters at St. Luke's. Mr B. N. Rayner was the licensed lay-reader for many years.

When the Rev. Heaton-Renshaw was vicar the church tower was struck by lightning, and rendered unsafe. I shall always remember the vicar walking nonchalantly round the scaffolding at the very top of the tower during the reconstruction. The church suffered damage during the 1939 war, in addition to the windows already mentioned, the south and east walls of the choir have been cracked, the portico damaged and the main doors were blown off. It also had to part with the iron railings and gates.

The small churchyard surrounding the church contains the graves of many departed parishioners, including that of my great-great-grandfather. A small portion of it was cut off in 1936 to make way for traffic improvements at the tram terminus.

A very pleasing war-time feature was the open-air concerts given in the churchyard during the summer by famous brass bands to an audience of people seated comfortably in deck chairs. This churchyard has now been made into a Garden of Remembrance in memory of Norwood men and women who gave their lives in the war of 1939–45. It was dedicated on the 23rd April, 1949, by the Lord Bishop of Southwark (the Right Rev. Bertram L. Simpson, M.C.) and was officially opened by Mr. Harold Bignold, president of the West Norwood branch of the British Legion. The names of the fallen are recorded in the Book of Remembrance placed in the West Norwood Library.

Of the many buildings connected with the church, St. Paul's in Elder Road, the parish hall, and St. Luke's Day Schools, I will speak as I come to them later.

Chapter 4
Norwood Cemetery

Just across the way from St. Luke's church is the South Metropolitan Cemetery, always referred to as Norwood Cemetery. An Act of Parliament (6 & 7 Will.4.C.cxxix) "for establishing a cemetery for the interment of the dead, southward of the Metropolis to be called the South Metropolitan Cemetery" was passed in 1837. The South Metropolitan Cemetery Company purchased the ground from the executors of Lord Thurlow, and the architect appointed was Sir William Tite, who built the Royal Exchange in London. There can be no doubt that under this eminent architect's planning a beautiful cemetery came into being. It is difficult to realise this now as one views the cemetery with its forest of white tombstones and monuments, how different the cemetery must have looked at the time when it was first opened. The green lawns, not divided into squares by straight roads, which to my mind gives an ugly uniformity, but by winding roads and paths, with clumps of trees here and there, the whole cemetery crowned by two imposing chapels built on the summit of the hill. Both these chapels are in the pointed style of English architecture, that for the Church of England being 70ft by 32ft and that for Nonconformists being slightly smaller, 60ft by 30ft.

The cemetery is entered through an imposing gateway, on one side of which are the arms of the See of Canterbury and on the other side the arms of the Diocese of Winchester in which the cemetery then was. It was the Bishop of Winchester who consecrated the cemetery on the 7th December 1837. The whole cemetery is surrounded by a remarkable wall nearly two miles in length, and built to a height of 12ft as a safeguard against body-snatchers, then prevalent. In its early days the company employed a night-watchman to guard against these unwholesome gentlemen, and the alarm rattle which this watchman carried on his rounds is still preserved in the offices of the company. Its sound can be heard for over half a mile. The wall is strengthened at intervals by massive brick buttresses, topped by stone cappings all carved with the same design with one exception. About half-way along the Robson Road wall there is one of these stone cappings with no carving at the sides. It is said that the masons who did the work believed in the old idea that it was an insult to Almighty God for mortal man to make anything perfect, so they left this stone incomplete as a symbol of their imperfection. The total cost of the cemetery was about £75,000. In addition to the main gateway there were other gates, one in the Norwood High Street is still used occasionally, but the one half way up the Auckland Hill wall and the one at the end of Hubbard Road have long been bricked up.

Under the original Act the cemetery company has to pay a fee for every interment in the Church of England portion of the cemetery to the incumbent of the parish (within a prescribed radius of the cemetery) in which the deceased person was a parishioner. Right down to the present day the burial registers of the company have to be kept open to the vicars of these parishes in order that they may collect these fees.

Norwood Cemetery is unique in that it has within its boundary walls two smaller cemeteries. The larger of these is the Greek Cemetery, covering almost exactly one acre and belonging to the Greek Church. This acre probably contains the remains of more millionaires than any acre of ground in England, for many wealthy Greek merchants and shipping magnates have their last resting-place there. Within its iron railings are enclosed many beautiful mausoleums and monuments, including the first marble monument to be erected in Norwood. The large Greek church in this cemetery was erected by the Ralli family in memory of their son who died at the early age of seventeen. This church has a very fine ceiling and the acoustic properties are marvellous; a whisper can be heard anywhere inside the building. Except for the re-opening of existing vaults and graves this little Greek cemetery is now full, and the Greek Church has purchased a similar plot in the Hendon Park Cemetery for future interments. The other small cemetery is the plot belonging to the church of St. Mary-at-Hill in the City of London. One of the original directors of the cemetery company was a churchwarden at this church, and as the burial ground attached to the church was nearly full it was at his suggestion that a portion of Norwood Cemetery became a sort of far-distant annexe to the churchyard of St. Mary-at-Hill. About 1892 alterations to the church resulted in several bodies being moved from the crypt to be re-interred in this plot in Norwood Cemetery, which, like the Greek Cemetery, is surrounded by iron railings.

Norwood was one of the first cemeteries to install a crematorium. A French firm, Toisal Fraudet of Paris, sent their workmen to build the first gas furnace, and the first cremation took place on the 13th May, 1915. Two more gas furnaces were subsequently added; they were of a new design patented by Mr. A. C. Lockwood, the then Secretary of the company. A columbarium was built in the annexe to the crematorium, with niches for the deposit of urns, and a small garden of rest is available for the scattering of ashes.

At the moment there are 40,000 graves in the cemetery, and nearly a quarter of a million people are buried there. A lady named Raincock had the doubtful distinction of being the first person to be buried there in 1837, and her grave which is Grave No. 1 was placed almost in the centre of the cemetery in Square 91. For the purposes of location the cemetery is divided into 125 squares, Square No. 1 being at the farthest corner of the cemetery over against Durban Road, the squares with the highest numbers being near the main entrance. The roads and paths have no official names, but they have been known by unofficial names given to them by generations of gravediggers and gardeners. These names are mostly taken from the principal grave adjacent to the road or path, e.g. Mackness Path, because the grave of Mr. Mackness, a former superintendent of the cemetery, is on the border of it. Another path is called Ship Path as on top of a monument by the side of the path is a beautiful model of a sailing ship carved in stone. At the corners of some of the paths stand small iron posts which, originally with chains hung between them, marked the boundary of the cemetery forecourt. The iron railings in front of the cemetery today were erected when a portion of the forecourt was cut off for road-widening about 40 years ago. In the forecourt stood the little "sentry-box" of the gate porter, who at one time wore a top-hat with gold braid round it. Many will remember Mr. Gusterson, who was the cemetery gate-porter for many years. On Sundays the gate-porter is kept busy loaning water-cans to visitors, and there are three small hand worked pumps in the cemetery for drawing water for these cans. Under both the church and chapel buildings are extensive catacombs containing many coffins, including those of some Belgian refugees who died here during the war of 1914–18. There are also many Germans buried in the cemetery in two small colonies of graves, due to the fact that there was a German church near Forest Hill.

In the days when any company of any standing had to have an office in the City the various companies owning cemeteries around London all had their City offices in addition to the small office at the cemetery itself. It was in 1936 that the South Metropolitan Cemetery Company, having purchased the ground adjoining the cemetery entrance, enlarged the office attached to the lodge and closed their offices in Temple Chambers.

There are not so many famous people buried in Norwood Cemetery as there are in some of the old North London cemeteries, but as the following list will show there are quite a number. Most famous of all is Spurgeon, the famous Baptist preacher, whose tomb is just in front of the Nonconformist Chapel. He died at Mentone in the South of France in 1892, and thousands attended his funeral at Norwood Cemetery; the committal service was conducted by the Rev. Archibald Brown. Dr. Robert Moffatt, the famous African Missionary, whose daughter married David Livingstone, is also buried at Norwood. The Law is represented by Lord Alverstone, Lord Chief Justice of England, Justice Talfourd and Sir Richard Muir. Politics by Sir Ernest Tritton and Mr. Thomas Lynn Bristowe,

both M.P.s for Norwood, Mr. George Harwood, M.P. for Bolton, and Sir Edwin Hall. Literature by Samuel Leman Blanchard (1845); Watts-Dunton (Swinburne's friend); Douglas Jerrold (1857), humorist and playwright, who contributed *Mrs. Caudle's Curtain Lectures* to *Punch* and who was editor of *Lloyds News*, Sir William Napier, the historian; and Sharon Turner, the historian of the Anglo-Saxons. Musicians include Sir Joseph Barnby and Sir August Manns, and the stage is represented by Paul Cinquevalli, the famous juggler; Mary Brough; Lionel Brough; Katti Lanner; George Conquest; Fred Robson, the comedian; Harriet Waylett (Kate Carney); George Bothwell Davidge; David Webster Obaldiston of the Surrey Theatre; and Alexander Lee, the composer, and manager of Drury Lane.

Sport is represented by three pugilists, Jack Purke; Tom King, champion of England, and Tom Spring (whose real name was Winter), also a champion of England.

I have a cutting from the *Morning Post* of the 16th May 1820 which reads:

"Boxing. There was a fine day's play on Epsom Downs yesterday in three fights, the first of which was between Spring and Robert Burn for 100 guineas a side. Spring is a first-rate scienced boxer, if not a smashing hitter."

It does not give the result of this fight.

Names famous in trade are also to be found in Norwood Cemetery: Jeremiah Colman (mustard); Sir Henry Tate (sugar); Sir Henry Doulton (china and pottery); James Epps (cocoa); Lawson Johnstone (Bovril); John Oakey (knife polish); Suttons (carriers); Cooks (of St. Paul's Churchyard); Stoughton (of Hodder & Stoughton, book publishers); and Higgs (of Higgs & Hill, building contractors). Two famous inventors lie here—Sir Henry Bessemer (1898), inventor of the steel process identified with his name. Also Sir Hiram Maxim, inventor of the Maxim machine-gun. Here also are two bankers, James W. Gilbart and Charles Whitburn, and two Lord Mayors of London, Sir Thomas Gabriel (Mayor 1866–7) and Sir Francis Truscott (Mayor 1879–80), with an engineer, Sir William Cubitt, and two Empire-builders, Sir William A'Beckett, First Chief Justice of Victoria, Australia, and Sir George Shenton, Governor-General of New South Wales, Australia. Here lie Henry Benjamin Beaufoy, who did so much for education in London, and three artists, Arthur "Crowquill" (Alfred Henry Forester, 1872), David Cox, painter in watercolours, who lived for some years in Dulwich, and Samuel Prout, Painter in Water-colours in Ordinary to George IV. Samuel Prout illustrated the works of John Britton (the antiquary), also buried in Norwood Cemetery. Here, too lies Gideon Mantell, geologist, discoverer of the Iguanodon and the Pterodactylus. Last but by no means least here is Mrs. Beeton of cookery book fame. Most people that I meet think of Mrs. Beeton as an old lady with curls, who boiled eggs in port wine and used half a pound of butter every time she fried a dish, but actually she was only 29 years of age when she died. A tiny tombstone near the Greek cemetery bears the inscription "Ada's pet Canary."

Norwood Cemetery suffered extensive damage during the late war, many high-explosive bombs having fallen in its grounds, damaging the walls and destroying hundreds of memorial stones. A flying-bomb badly damaged the crematorium and another demolished the offices and the entrance lodge, where Mr. Francis Nice, superintendent for the past 40 years, had a narrow escape. The blast from this bomb also badly damaged the mausoleum erected in recent years by Dr. Maddicks, close to the entrance.

Galer in his book, *Norwood and Dulwich*, page 20, says:

"It is hard to decide whether the presence of such a large burying ground in the midst of so thickly populated a district as Norwood is not prejudicial to the health of the inhabitants, but it is an open question whether the large suburban cemeteries such as those at Norwood and Nunhead will not have to be moved further afield."

Well, that was written 60 years ago, and Norwood Cemetery is still open for burials. Neither does the neighbourhood appear to be unhealthy, quite the reverse.

Chapter 5
Norwood Road

I now propose to take my reader for a walk along the roads and streets of Norwood, pausing to recall old places which have long since disappeared and to bring back to mind the people associated with them. I propose to start from the very centre of Norwood, the present tram terminus, so "Shall we gather at the Fountain" which stands there. This fountain was erected in 1897 to the memory of Mrs. Woodford Fawcett who used to hold temperance meetings on the spot where it stands, outside the main gates of St. Luke's Church. From this fountain let us walk down the right hand (or Dulwich) side of Norwood Road as far as Brockwell Park, and from there we will return along the other side (the Streatham side) pausing to consider the various side roads as we go. Norwood Road has changed with the years more than any other road in Norwood. A hundred years ago it was narrow, somewhat muddy and unlit, with only a few large houses here and there. There were no side roads at all leading towards Dulwich from the cemetery right down to Herne Hill. The only approach to Dulwich was by footpaths across the fields. From the Tulse Hill Hotel to Herne Hill it was only a very rough muddy track called Norwood Lane. The main road to Brixton being over Tulse Hill, this lane was very quiet and unfrequented.

Commencing from the cemetery entrance the first building we reach is the "Thurlow Arms", a public house named after Lord Thurlow, of whom I will speak later. The Thurlow Arms once had extensive stabling at the side, and a horse trough in its forecourt. By the side of the Thurlow Arms Robson Road runs along the side of the cemetery wall, and is always referred to by old inhabitants as "Cemetery Wall" and not as Robson Road. Originally it was called Park Road from the "Thurlow Arms" to the "Alleyn's Head". The part alongside the cemetery wall was later given the separate name of Robson Road after Mr. Robson, the first superintendent of Norwood Cemetery.

Where Robson Road ends and Park Road (now Park Hall Road) begins, stands a house, at the corner of the cemetery wall. This house had until 1938 a large ornamental gateway at the side of it. This gateway was surmounted by the Royal Arms. About 1830 the house was occupied by a Mr. Herring, known throughout Europe as a dealer and collector of "wild and fancy" animals, birds, and fish. In the garden he had a private zoo, including an artificial lake stocked with goldfish. One of the highest buildings recently demolished was the house in which the giraffes were kept. Many stories are told of the alarm caused in this quiet country spot, as it then was, when a new arrival roared throughout the night, and an occasional escape set the neigh-

bourhood on tenterhooks. The Royal Arms were erected on the gateway about 1835 when William IV granted Mr. Herring a charter for the supply of golden pheasants. Four years later, two years after her accession, Queen Victoria granted a second charter for the supply of goldfish to the Court. These charters are I believe still in possession of the owner of the property. After Mr. Herring left the house efforts were made by the authorities from time to time to have the coat of arms removed, but the only serious threat was when Mr. Green, the jobmaster, occupied the premises. An official who demanded the removal was told that those who put the arms there were responsible for taking them down, and anyway the carved stone formed an integral part of the arch, and could not be touched without weakening the structure. From that day no further protests were made.

Before we leave this part of Park Hall Road I must mention the big old houses between this house and the corner of Rosendale Road. Some of these have already been demolished to make way for the block of flats at the corner of Martell Road, and for the new Gipsy Hill telephone exchange. The West Dulwich Congregational Church stood at the corner of Chancellor Road (now Grove). The Rev. C. F. W. Wood, M.A., the Rev. W. Tarbox, and the Rev. R. C. Sandison were ministers longest associated with this church, which was totally destroyed by bomb blast in 1940. Further along Park Hall Road, where is now Clive Road, stood Rosendale Hall, a lovely old manor house formerly called Hall Place or Knowles. A house marked "Mr. Wheller" on Rocque's map seems to denote this old mansion. Hall's *History of Dulwich* (page 5, second edition, 1922) says:

"From the south end of Gallery Road, a track led southwards across the common to the Manor House, known in 1541 as Hall Place, built chiefly of timber, standing close to what is now Park Hall Road, nearly opposite the end of Croxted Road. It had been the summer residence of the Abbots of Bermondsey and later on was the residence of Edward Alleyn, the founder of Dulwich College. In 1750 a Captain Lynn lived there, and in a quarrel with a neighbour, resulting in a duel close by, the Captain was killed. In 1768 the then tenant partially rebuilt the house and so it remained until 1883 when it was pulled down to the great regret of many. It stood in grounds of about 30 acres, extending towards Gipsy Hill. The track from Back Lane to the manor house was converted by the same tenant, in 1773, into a road, practically identical with that part of the present Alleyn Park which is on the west of the College playing-fields."

Having paused to review Robson and Park Hall Roads let us return to the "Thurlow Arms" and continue our walk along Norwood Road. Next to the public house are four shops to the corner of Chestnut

Road. The first is the old-established builder's merchants, E. Vincent & Son. Fifty years ago the other shops were occupied by North's, drapers; Cousins's, grocers; and a branch of the London and South Western Bank. Chestnut Road had the remains of an iron gate at this end of it at one time. Was it once a private road, or was this the remains of the turnpike gate that stood across Norwood Road at this point? A small hall a few yards along the right-hand side of Chestnut Road, now used by Messrs. Vincent as a store, was called the Conference Hall, where Mrs. Woodford Fawcett also held temperance meetings. There were only a few houses in Chestnut Road, some large houses at the Norwood Road end, and one standing on its own further down. For many years now the reluctant feet of Norwood's schoolchildren have been drawn, usually under promises of sweets, etc., if they are good, to the first house on the left, which is the L.C.C. school treatment centre. As we pass along the row of shops from Chestnut Road to the corner of Chatsworth Road let us call to mind the names of the old tradesmen associated with them. First at the corner of Chestnut Road was the Syndicate Stores of Mr. Rowland Ellis, now Williamson's. Then came Bennett's depository; Haile's, provisions; Mr. Burley, draper; Mr. F. Griffiths, butcher; River's, boot stores; Sewell, chemist; Taylor, ironmonger; and Mr. W. N. Willoughby, auction offices. In more recent years the progressive firm of Messrs. E. H. Day & Son have rebuilt and occupied some of these premises, at the back of which the firm also built their extensive furniture depositories in 1923.

When Chatsworth Road Baptist Church was first built it was surrounded by fields. Early in 1876 some friends in Norwood were led to express a strong desire that a Baptist cause should be established among them, and Mr. Thomas Spurrier wrote to seek the assistance of the Rev. J. T. Wigner, President of the London Baptist Association. A site was secured at a cost of £500, and the building was begun on the 20th October, 1876. The cornerstone was laid on November 21st of that year by the Rev. J. T. Wigner. I have seen the ornamental wooden mallet which was used; it was presented to Mr. Spurrier, whose daughter, Mrs. Palmer of Auckland Hill, has it still. The cost of the chapel, including the site and the small lecture hall which then stood at the rear, was about £6,000 which was increased to £7,400 by the addition of galleries and the erection of boundary walls. The chapel was opened on Tuesday, 11th December, 1877. The Rev. C. H. Spurgeon had been announced to preach but was taken ill and his place was taken by the Rev. J. T. Wigner. At the beginning of 1878 Mr. Wigner was greatly concerned about obtaining a suitable minister, and ultimately wrote to ask the Rev. William Fuller Gooch, of Falmouth, to occupy tbe pulpit for a Sunday or two. He was then unanimously invited to become the minister, and commenced his ministry on 24th March 1878 with a church membership of 26. So effective was his preaching and work that the 26 had grown to 500 members by 1892, in which year Mr. Gooch

resigned because he had felt for some time the strain of denominational ties. He longed for more freedom in the work of preaching the Gospel. Of his subsequent ministry in Norwood I will write later, for it concerns Lansdowne Hall church. The Rev. James L. Stanley succeeded Mr. Gooch on June 13th, 1892, and went to Muller's Homes at Bristol in July 1897. Then the Rev. Archibald G. Brown, of the East London Tabernacle, accepted the call to Chatsworth on September 24th, 1897. He carried on a wonderful ministry for ten years until he went to a larger sphere of work at the Metropolitan Tabernacle. For the next 17 years the pastor was the Rev. David John Hiley who had carried on a big work at Bristol. In the war of 1914-18, Mr. Hiley served as Chaplain to the Canadian Forces in France. After the war Mr. Hiley resigned, and afterwards went to Muswell Hill. The Rev. H. J. Galley, a man of fine preaching ability, was the next pastor for some seven or eight years before leaving for Bath. He was followed by the Rev. E. W. Mills, who was succeeded by the Rev. F. A. Goodwin. The church, together with the fine Sunday School halls (which were built in 1900 at a cost of £6,000 to replace the original lecture hall) was totally destroyed in September 1944 by one of the first V2 rockets to fall in London. Worship was then carried on at the Knight's Hill Wesleyan Church and the West Norwood Brotherhood Hall until a temporary church was opened on the old site in October, 1947. In 1945 when workmen were clearing the remains of the main tower they found under the foundation stone a cavity in which the original officers of the church had deposited a glass container sealed with red lead, containing records of the Baptist community of 1876.

Between Chatsworth Road and Lancaster Avenue there stood three big old houses with carriage drives—Frensham Lodge, Quebec Lodge and Clarendon Lodge. They were demolished to make way for the fine row of shops known as The Broadway, built by Mr. Maley. Tradesmen whose names are remembered in The Broadway shops are: Mr. Yeo, china and glass; Sheldrick, electrician; Craven & Co., pianoforte manufacturers; Blay, tailor; Salter, chemist; and Swaddling's, toys and games. The late Mr. J. Watson did a large amount of building in the Chestnut Road and Chatsworth Way area. He came from Ardlui in Scotland, and Ardlui Road owes its name to this fact. On the corner of Norwood Road and Lancaster Avenue, where a modern block of flats now stands, was a rather dingy-looking house called Thurlow House, the residence of a family named Potier. Between this house and the fire station are some more modern red brick houses, one of which was the residence of Dr. Sandeman. The fire station was opened at the beginning of the 1914-18 war, and maroons were fired from the tower to give warnings of air raids. Next to the fire station is the tram depot of the London Passenger Transport Board.

Next to the tram depot is what I think must be the oldest house in Norwood. It is marked on Rocque's map as Knight's Hill Farm, and was later known as Thurlow Lodge and now as Serbia House.

Knight's Hill was presumably named after a family of that name. On 13th April, 1487, John Knight, husbandman, of Knyghts Hill in Lambhithe, made his will. John was evidently a prosperous farmer, owning lands at Knight's Hill, Streatham and Lewisham. Eighteen years later we have the will of Henry Knight of Knyghtes Hill in the parish of Lambhithe. Presumably he was the third son of John Knight and, his elder brothers having died, he became the heir. He desired, like his father before him, to be buried in Lambeth churchyard. How Knight's Hill descended after this we don't know, but before the middle of the 16th century it belonged to Hugh Knight. Although Rocque's map of London shows Knight's Hill Farmhouse, it does not show the hill between Norwood Road and Rosendale Road (opposite Brockwell Park). It shows Knight's Hill a mile to the South, where the present Knight's Hill is. But the map of Lambeth Manor, 1806, engraved by E. Driver (in the Minet Library Roll 1) does show this hill near Herne Hill as Knight's Hill; it was of course on the Knight's Hill farm estate.

This Knight's Hill farm estate covered practically the whole of the area between the present Croxted and South Croxted Roads, the Norwood Road, the Norwood High Street and Gipsy Road.

The name Thurlow Lodge was after Lord Thurlow, whose name is also commemorated by Thurlow Park Road, Thurlow Hill, the "Thurlow Arms", and Chancellor Grove, for Lord Thurlow was the Lord Chancellor of England. The part of Norwood Road where this house stands was once called Thurlow Place. Lord Thurlow's coat-of-arms can still be seen over the main doorway of the "Thurlow Arms". Lord Thurlow was born in 1730 and died 1806, and it was said that "no one was ever so wise as Thurlow looked." He purchased Brockwell Green Farm in 1785, the Manor of Leigham Court in 1789, and at various times other land in this district.

Lord Chancellor Thurlow employed Henry Holland, the architect of old Drury Lane Theatre, to build him a house. The mansion was finished and much admired. A splendid prospect was visible from the upper rooms. The grounds also were extensive and beautiful. Strange to relate, however, his Lordship refused to occupy his mansion, and persisted in living in the inferior house of Knight's Hill farm adjoining (Serbia House). Let me here quote what Lord Chancellor Eldon said about this:—

"Lord Thurlow built a house in the neighbourhood of London. Now he was first cheated by his architect and then he cheated himself. For the house cost more than he expected so he would never go into it. Very foolish but so it was. As he was coming out of the Queen's drawing-room a lady whom I knew very well stopped him and asked him when he was going into his new house. 'Madam' said he, 'the Queen has just asked me that impudent question and as I would not tell her I will not tell you'."

The mansion stood behind Serbia House, between the present Elmcourt Road and Lancaster Avenue, near Thurlow Park Road. It was at right-angles to Norwood Road, i.e. the front faced north, and between it and Serbia House were the gardens of the mansion.

After Thurlow's death an Act was passed in 1808 enabling his executors to pull down the mansion and sell the land.

Even if it had no connection with Lord Thurlow, Serbia House would still be worthy of mention for forty years ago it was the residence of Sir Hiram Maxim, the inventor of the machine-gun that bears his name. From this house in Norwood Road Sir Hiram sent a letter to the *Norwood Press* informing the public that he would be experimenting with his gun in the garden and if people kept their windows open there would be no danger of broken glass. It was in this garden that his first fixed "flying-machine" was erected, and the local public were invited in for trial flights. It was really a series of boats on the merry-go-round principle, and the faster the machine in the middle went, the higher the boats, on flexible wires, flew. Maxim's flying machine was a feature of the sports gound at the Crystal Palace, where it still stands. Sir Hiram was always busy at something. He invented a patent pipe for asthma sufferers, and during the 1914-18 war he started a factory packing pork and beans for the troops. He was a clever cartoonist, and had an intense dislike for clergymen and missionaries. During Sir Hiram's residence his home had massive gates with gun-metal handles, and American eagles surmounted the stone pillars of the gateway. Sir Hiram took these gates with him when he moved to Ryecoats, Dulwich Common, where he died in 1916 aged 76. The American eagles are still there. In tbe 1914-18 war Maxim's Norwood home was the home of some Serbian refugees, and its name was changed from Thurlow Lodge to Serbia House.

Between this house and Court Road (now Elmcourt Road) stood first, two villas, Louvaine Villa and Clifton Villa (both still there), and at the corner, where the block of flats now stands, was Pagoda Lodge. From Elmcourt Road to the railway bridge were three large houses, Thurlow Place, residence of Lady Grey; Bervie House; and Libton House (J. M. Yetts). One of these houses was the Constitutional Club, and one was Veryard and Yates's estate office, destroyed by a flying-bomb in 1944. The road beside this house is Avenue Park Road, though with the railway and railway wharf on one side of it and some mediocre houses on the other side of it, the name Avenue Park seems almost a jest. In Avenue Park Road is Maley Avenue, named after Mr. Maley who built many houses in that area, and who also built that fine row of shops, between Chatsworth Road and Lancaster Avenue, known as The Broadway.

Whenever one thinks of the row of shops from the railway bridge to Tulse Hill station approach the personality who comes foremost to mind is that remarkable old gentleman Mr. William Redpath, the chemist and postmaster whose business was established in 1870. In 1935 Mr. Redpath received the King's Jubilee medal for 62 years' service as

Postmaster. In April 1944 the following appeared in the national daily newspapers: "William Redpath, war evacuee from West Norwood, who spent his 100th birthday in Capetown, South Africa yesterday said: 'I want to get back to London, bombs or no bombs'." Mr. Redpath, however, died in South Africa in his 101st year. Other tradesmen whose names come to mind in connection with this row of shops, once called Thurlow Terrace, are Mr. Malyon, gent's outfitter; Baylis, auctioneer; Turpin, ironmongery; Kirby, draper; the Misses Hamburger, wool and fancy needlework; Mr. John William Jones, grocery and wine stores; and Mr. Curtis, butcher, afterwards Briginshaw & Boys. In Approach Road, now Station Rise, are some more old-established businesses. In 1861 Mr. Henry Kemp from Bromley began supplying post horses and private carriages at the stables of the "Thurlow Arms", but with the coming of the Brighton Railway to Tulse Hill in 1867 he secured a site next to the station, and built stables there. The business was carried on by Mr. Kemp and his son Mr. Stephen Kemp until 1892, when it was sold to Mr. Stepple and in 1906 it was sold again to Messrs. Tye of Forest Hill. Mr. F. J. Lockwood was for many years a watch and clock maker in a shop adjoining. Mrs. Lockwood was a daughter of Mr. Kemp: they lived to celebrate their golden wedding. Warrens, the coal merchants of Broad Street, have had a branch office there for over 60 years.

From Station Rise to Thurlow Park Road were some big houses, some of which are still standing. The houses from Thurlow Park Road to St. Faith's Road are more recent. One is the South London Botanical Institute, with the kindly Mr. Sherrin as principal.

I have already spoken of the loneliness of Norwood Lane as it was called from Tulse Hill Hotel to Herne Hill. Most of the Dulwich side of it was covered with two brickfields, King's, which stretched from St. Faith's Road to Trinity Rise, and Thompson's, on the site of the present Peabody Buildings, Rosendale Road. Brickmaking was quite a local industry a hundred years ago, and most of the older buildings in Norwood, including my own home, were built with bricks made in the locality. Old Norwood residents will remember the heaps of red rubble on the site of the present Glennie Road district and also on Auckland Hill, which was called locally the Red Hill, because of it. There were some little one-storied timber-built cottages by the Tulse Hill to Herne Hill railway viaduct occupied by brickfield workers. The hill known as Knight's Hill, behind these cottages, which I have mentioned before, is partly natural and partly artificial, a lot of clay being deposited on to it during the excavations for the railways from Tulse Hill to Herne Hill and North Dulwich. The ground is unsuitable for building owing to the shifting nature of the soil, and during the summer months big cracks and fissures appear in its surface during very dry weather. The railway line from Tulse Hill to Herne Hill has been blocked at times by landslides.

I said earlier that there were no roads leading towards Dulwich from Norwood Road, and that the only approach to Dulwich was by footpaths. I will so far correct that statement by saying that towards Herne Hill there was a winding track, too large to be called a footpath, but not large enough to be called a road, called Croxted Lane. It is marked on Rocque's map as Crocksted Lane, and a photograph of it taken as late as 1875 shows what a rural lane it was then. Near to the corner of it in Norwood Road stood Perrin's timber yard with a small house. Where the long row of lock-up shops is now, between Croxted Road and Herne Hill railway bridge, was Riley's Rustic Works.

This completes our walk along the Dulwich side of Norwood Road.

Let us now cross over to the other side and walk back to West Norwood again. Opposite to where Croxted Road joins Norwood Road is Brockwell Park. This park was the estate of Brockwell Hall, a rather dreary looking 19th century building which is now the refreshment room. In 1789 the old manor house was a handsome white house belonging to Thomas Cole, merchant, who sold it to John Ogbourne who, in 1809, sold it to John Blades, a sheriff of the City of London. Blades pulled down the old Brockwell Hall and built the present house. In 1829 the estate descended to Blades's son-in-law, John Blades Blackburn, in whose family it remained until it was bought for the public. That it became a public park is a credit to the public spirit of a few men of vision who saw what Herne Hill would look like within a generation or so. The leader was Thomas Lynn Bristowe, the first M.P. for Norwood, who, in the face of considerable difficulties, fought to save the estate from the builder. The money was eventually collected, and the first portion, consisting of 81 acres, was acquired at a cost of £120,000. Subsequent additions acquired at a cost of nearly £71,000 have increased its area to 127½ acres. The opening ceremony was performed by the Earl of Rosebery in June 1892, and on that day Mr. Bristowe saw his dream come true, but alas, he was taken ill almost immediately after the opening ceremony, collapsing into the arms of Alderman John Williams. He died within a very few minutes of heart failure. Near the Herne Hill entrance is a memorial in the form of a drinking fountain surmounted by a bust of Mr. Bristowe. The inscription on the column reads: "Ready for every good work he led the movement for the acquisition of these broad acres as a public park with great tact and energy, and died suddenly at the very moment of his unselfish triumph at the opening of the park on Whit Monday 1892." The great feature of the Park is the Old Garden. Someone had the brilliant inspiration to make the walled kitchen garden of the Old Hall into a typical Old English garden, filled not with vegetables, but with flowers. This garden was so popular that it became, so to speak, the parent of all the other Old English gardens in the L.C.C. parks. A particular feature of the old-world garden is the model Kentish village, constructed and presented by Mr. Edgar Wilson, aged 76 years, of Hamilton Road, West Norwood. A similar village has been presented by Mr. Wilson to the City of Melbourne, Australia, in appreciation of the brotherly aid received by our old people from the people of Australia. The turret clock in Brockwell Park, a facsimile of the one outside Victoria Station, bears the inscription: "The gift of Charles Ernest Tritton, Member of Parliament for Norwood, 1879." The flagstaff near the refreshment house bears a brass plate worded: "The gift of Charles Ernest Tritton, M.P. for Norwood, Coronation Day, 26th June, 1902." The ponds in Brockwell Park besides being the meeting place of local model yacht enthusiasts were also the rendezvous of early morning swimmers. In July 1937 the open air swimming bath was opened. Some fine performances have been given at the open air theatre opened in the Park under the "Holidays at Home" scheme.

Between Brockwell Park and the Tulse Hill Hotel the oldest building is the Westmoreland Society's School, a picturesque building now hidden behind garage premises. This school originated in the Westmoreland Society, which was founded in London in 1746 to afford a means of uniting natives of Westmoreland then living in or near London, and above all to assist young men coming to London from that county in their efforts to earn a living. The Society does not seem to have accomplished a great deal until 1810, when the second Earl of Lonsdale became president. It was decided to build a school for children of Westmoreland parents residing within 75 miles of London. By 1850 the building fund had reached £3,712, and about that time a Mrs. Edwards offered an acre of land at Tulse Hill on very advantageous terms. On May 4th 1852 the foundation stone of the school was laid, and the buildings were opened on the 17th January 1854. Five years later the school was enlarged. The privileges of the school were not limited to orphans; the only condition was that at least one of the parents must have been born in Westmoreland. The grounds of the school covered the area at the back of Trinity Rise near the top of which is Holy Trinity Church.

The parish of Holy Trinity was separated from the parish of St. Luke in 1855, and the foundation stone of the church was laid in that year by Sir Charles Crossley, Sheriff of London. The building was completed a year later at a cost of £7,500, which included the adjoining vicarage. The building is of Kentish rag stone, and is designed in the early Geometric Decorated style. Its chief architectural features are the wide span of the nave, with its remarkable timbered roof, and the graceful spire which rises nearly 90 feet above the main building. The nave is designed to accommodate 1,000 persons. The day schools were built by public subscription in Lutheran Place about 1870, and have remained in the control of the church managers. In 1944 they were entirely destroyed by enemy action, but plans are afoot for their replacement. The daughter church of St. John in Guernsey Grove was erected in 1911, and is an attractive little church with a spacious hall underneath. The past Vicars of Holy Trinity Church include: The Rev. W. C. Moore,

who died at the vicarage and is buried in Norwood Cemetery. He was succeeded by the Rev. E. L. Roxby, M.A., a scholarly and devout preacher with a great interest in the work of foreign missions. Then came the Rev. Henry W. Wolfindin, M.A., who died after leaving for another sphere of work. His wife was a daughter of the Rev. W. C. Moore. The Rev. Montague Dale was vicar for many years, and was made a canon a short time before he left. The present vicar, the Rev. Canon T. G. Edwards, M.A., was formerly vicar of Emmanuel Church, Clive Road, West Dulwich. The late Dr. Walmsley Little, F.R.C.O., was for many years organist and choirmaster.

The Tulse Hill Hotel, built in 1840, is pretty much the same now, though the forecourt is a wee bit smaller, and the horse trough has gone. At the side of it is Tulse Hill, once, as we have seen, the main road from Norwood to Brixton. The unusual name Tulse is from a family of that name, first found in the parish 1656, Feet of Fines at the Public Record Office. Sir Henry Tulse was Lord Mayor of London in 1684. He was at one time Master of the Ancient Society of College Youths (the Society of Bellringers). He is buried in the churchyard of St. Dionis Backchurch, Lime Street, E.C. The blocks of flats on the new L.C.C. housing estate on Tulse Hill are named after the Masters, Members, and other persons connected with the Ancient Society of College Youths, as follows:—

Bartell House—Edward Bartell, a gentleman ringer of the Society.

Birch House—Samuel Birch an eminent member on the roll of the Society.

Booth House—Henry Booth, a member of the Society who rang a peal at St. Matthew's, Bethnal Green, 27th April, 1868.

Brereton House—Lord Brereton one of the Founders of the Society and the first Master in 1637.

Cherry Close—R. R. Cherry, Lord Chief Justice of Ireland, a member of the Society in the 19th century.

Dearmer House—John Dearmer, one of the ringers in the first peal of Bob Maximus ever rung, 26th Feb. 1726.

Ellacombe House—Rev. H. T. Ellacombe, M.A., F.S.A., author of The Church Bells of Devon.

Greenleaf Close—Wm. Greenleaf, one of the ringers of the first peal of Stedman Caters, 8th December, 1883.

Hardham House—John Hardham, member of the Society.

Haworth House—J. R. Haworth, one of the ringers of the first complete peal rung in Ireland 27th July 1872.

Heywood House—Sir A. P. Heywood, Bart., eminent member of the Society.

Holdsworth House—Joseph Holdsworth, one of Osborn's list of College Youths.

Lansdell House—Edward S. Lansdell, one of the ringers of a peal of Stedman Cinques at St. Michael's, Cornhill, 27th April, 1861.

2

3

4

5

7

6

8

9

10

11

12

13

14

15

16

Laughton House—Will Laughton one of the earliest writers about bell-ringers.

Lomley House—Sir Martin Lomley, member of the Society.

Povey House—John Povey, a member of the Society.

Purser House—James Purser, one of the ringers of a peal at Shoreditch Town in 1788.

Rudhall House—Abraham Rudhall, a bell founder of Gloucester.

Scarsbrook House—G. Scarsbrook, one of the ringers of a peal at Southwark Cathedral in 1802.

Stedman Close—Fabian Stedman dedicated his *Campanalogia* to the Society of which he was a member, 1677.

Tendring House—John Tendring, through whom double changes in ringing came into practice. Master in 1659.

Washbrook House—J. W. Washbrook, a member of the Society.

Woodruff House—William Woodruff, one of the twelve College Youths who rang the first peal of Grandsire Cinques on 19th January, 1724.

The row of shops between the Tulse Hill Hotel and Romola Road call to mind the names of the tradesmen: Maclaren, butcher; Brake, baker; Maley, builder; and Cropthall, oil and colour stores. At the corner of Tulse Hill and Norwood Road opposite to the Tulse Hill Hotel was a large private residence with a lawn and tall trees. I have been told, but have been unable to confirm, that Mr. Gladstone once visited the owners of this house and witnessed a demonstration of a tree-felling machine patented by the firm of Ransome and Rapiers. The site of this house is now covered by the row of shops called the Quadrant. Well-known occupiers of these shops are: H. Parker, grocer; Evans, tailor; Crown Laundry; M. Philcox & Savidge, jewellers; J. T. Cook, boot stores; Taylor's household stores; Vinden, greengrocer; and Cox's bakery. Between Perran Road and Christchurch Road were the shops of McMillan, draper; Wilson Harris, library; and Charrington's, coal. Christchurch Road, like Tulse Hill, has many fine residences, the largest is Fenstanton, an imposing house with a wonderful hall and staircase; its grounds run down to Perran Road. At the corner of Christchurch Road and Norwood Road stands the beautiful Roupell Park Wesleyan church. Built in 1879, I have read that when it was completed and before the scaffolding was taken down the late Mr. John Peed and two or three more of the church officers climbed right to the top and sang the doxology. Many fine mass meetings have been held in this church. On one occasion General William Booth, the founder of the Salvation Army, gave an address on "Darkest England and the way out". Another mass meeting was addressed by Frances Willard, founder of the White Ribbon movement in America. Other functions held there included meetings of the Norwood Literature, Science and Art Society. Dr. A. J. Rice-Oxley (afterwards knighted for services to royalty) was one of its moving spirits. Attending the lectures regularly afforded a liberal education. Among lectures given were H. M. Stanley on "How I found Livingstone", Sir Robert Ball on "Astronomy", Dr. Nansen on "The First crossing of Greenland", and Colonel Gourard, Edison's representative, on "The Phongraph" (Phonograph). Many ministers have served the church, among the best known being the Rev. John Kinnings and the Rev. George Bainbridge. Next to the church, where the row of shops called The Parade now stands, stood Duffield House Academy, a school for young ladies. The Parade shops were occupied by Frisby, outfitter; Grimes, draper; and Francis, grocery and provisions. At the corner of Palace Road was the old house and nursery of Mr. John Peed. This old established business bears the arms of a royal appointment. It has been carried on by the son and grandson of the founder. Another son manages the Mitcham Lane nurseries. Palace Road used to be a private road throughout its length with wooden gates at each end. Today only the portion from Hillside Road to Streatham Hill is private, with notice boards by the gates at each end saying that funerals and other objectionable traffic are forbidden. There you may still see the old watchman, employed by the residents, with his top hat with faded gold braid, sweeping up the leaves with his birch broom.

Roupell Park Church and Roupell Road are named after an estate which covered the Hillside Road area. Richard Palmer Roupell, a wealthy lead merchant, purchased this estate and gave it the name of Roupell Park. The house was a large towered mansion locally called the Grotto by the corner of Hillside Road, with ornamental gardens which were open to the public. Richard P. Roupell had for some years cohabited with a woman by whom he had several children, one of whom was a son William. Richard Roupell eventually married the woman and they had another son after the marriage to whom he gave his own name, and as the law stood then, this son was the only legitimate child. William, who was the favourite son, was ignorant of his illegitimacy, and being his father's chief business adviser, not unnaturally conceived that he would one day inherit this estate. He defrauded his father of £10,000, and then according to his confession, forged at least ten deeds which he secretly negotiated, and raised the enormous sum of £150,000, of which during the lifetime of his father he expended £70,000 on the improvement of the Roupell Park estate. At length, the father, feeling that his end was near informed William of the circumstances of his birth. William was thunderstruck. It meant that the estate would go to the only legitimate son, and all William's frauds and forgeries would be discovered. As soon as his father died, he came to the house, took possession of his father's will, and at once forged another. He thus became possessed of enormous property, and obtained the social position which the possession of riches commands. He stood for Parliament and by lavish expenditure became M.P. for Lambeth in 1857. Eventually he ran through the fortune, and feeling that his crimes were bound to come to light, fled the country. He afterwards came back to meet the charges, and was tried before Mr. Justice Byles at the Central Criminal Court. He was sentenced to penal servitude for life. A fuller account of his life and election to Parliament can be read in *The Electoral History of the Borough of Lambeth* by George Hill.

Before leaving the Palace Road district, I would like to mention a lady renowned for her good works, Mrs. Donald Campbell. She was the founder of the Hitherfield Road Free Church off Leigham Vale, and was an ardent supporter of all religious and temperance work in the district. She was also a founder of a branch of the Y.W.C.A. in Norwood, and of the Norwood Crèche.

Passing under the railway bridge, we come to a modern row of shops with the Temperance Billiard Hall over them. In connection with this site I came across the following statement in a book called *Picturesque Dulwich and Vicinity* published by Messrs. Phibbs Gibson & Co., in 1898–9.

"... is the site to be devoted to the proposed new Town Hall, which from the designs drawn up by Messrs. Boughton & Son, the architects entrusted with the business, will be such a fine building as to cause discontent in many of the surrounding suburbs which are not quite so up to date as Norwood."

Whether it was ever intended to build a town hall here or not I cannot say; I merely include this paragraph as a matter of interest. I do not believe everything I read in print, and nowhere have I been able to confirm this extraordinary statement.

From the railway bridge at Tulse Hill to a point where the Regal Cinema now stands were many large houses, occupied by City gentlemen. Only three of these remain today. One is occupied by Messrs. Lane's garage. Next door is Mr. Mark, the builder, whose father Mr. Walter Mark was also a builder there. The third house is behind the Lancaster Motor Garage, but this will shortly be pulled down as it was badly burned in an air raid during 1944. This latter house was once the residence of the popular comedian of his day, Mr. Charles Godfrey, who was very proud of his garden.

The houses from the railway bridge to Harpenden Road were known locally as "The African Village". Between Harpenden Road and York Hill stood a two-storied wooden-framed house in the early American style, which stood in wooded grounds with an orchard at the rear. This house was called Willow Lodge and was the residence of Dr. Chapman, who had for his partner Dr. Moon, father of the present Dr. Moon. From Harpenden Road a roadway runs behind the present Salvation Army Hall into one of Norwood's little known backwaters, Penrith Place, consisting of two villas and several dwellings over coach-houses, reached by wooden outside staircases. There is a similar colony at the side of John Peed's nursery, called Parade Mews. In Ullswater Road opposite Ulverstone Road was the little Willoughby Hall, originally the furniture saleroom of Mr. Willoughby, the auctioneer, and later the scene of many local dances and other social functions. It was afterwards the 12th Church of Christ Scientist. On the corner opposite to this Hall was the Anglo-German School of Music. Founded in Norwood Road by Miss Emily Upton, afterwards Mrs. Upton-Dene, when she married Otto Dene the tenor vocalist. The pupils gave concerts at the old Public Hall on Knight's Hill. Mrs. Dene went to Canada and established a school in Toronto, but Mr. Dene having died there she returned to England. In 1930 she married Mr. Krause, a violin master, and they re-opened the school of music, retiring to Bournemouth in 1934. In York Road (now York Hill) was Gressan Hall, residence of Mr. Christmas, partner in the provision firm of Lovell and Christmas. On the left side of York Hill is York Hall, the headquarters of the British Legion in Norwood. These premises have been badly damaged by bombing as have all the other houses in this much bombed road.

At the top of York Hill where it joins Royal Circus stood Tonge House, residence of the Portal family. This family could trace their pedigree back a long way, Sir Gerald de Portal was plenipotentiary on a mission to Menelik, Abyssinia, a generation or two ago. Mr. Richard Brinsley Portal first came to Tonge House, and after his death, his son, William R. Portal and his two sisters continued to occupy the house until death claimed them one by one. They were great benefactors to St. Luke's Church. In addition to the Portal screen to the Lady Chapel I have already mentioned, Miss Portal gave the carved oak organ casing which was dedicated by the Bishop of Southwark, 23rd June, 1933. The family also instituted the Portal Homes erected in Royal Circus in 1937. The back of Tonge House, which was pulled down in 1937, was much more imposing that the front, and its garden stretched down to the corner of Knollys Road. A small road named Cambrian Close now covers the site of this garden.

Next door to Tonge House in Royal Circus stood Cambrian House, also pulled down in 1937. The little road which now stands on its site is called Portal Close. Surely the names of these two roads should have been the other way round.

Even the name Royal Circus is a puzzle, for as far as I can make out, it was never visited by Royalty. Its original name was York Crescent. It is also hard to understand why it was thought necessary to spend nearly £600 to make this quiet road a one-way street.

On the circular piece of ground enclosed by this road stands the Portal Homes, erected in 1937. Fifty years ago it was known as Luck's Farm. Mr. Luck, who used to drive round Norwood selling milk from his cart, lived in an old cottage with extensive meadow land at the rear. A modern villa now stands where the old cottage stood.

The meadow land was known as High View Park, the ground of the West Norwood Football Club, nicknamed "The Bantams" because most of the players were small. Under the presidency of Sir Ernest Tritton, M.P., the club prospered and eventually won many trophies, including the London Senior Cup, London Charity Cup, etc. Such famous teams as Preston North End, Tottenham Hotspur,

West Bromwich Albion, Bristol City, Millwall, Old Carthusians and Plymouth Argyle played on the ground at High View Park. When West Norwood F.C. was at its zenith, Dulwich Hamlet were juniors, with "Pa" Wilson as president. It is now one of the leading amateur clubs. The founders and players of West Norwood Football Club were the brothers Sid and Roger Thompson, J. W. Pryce, Tom Pryce, Freddie Holford, R. Blythe, J. Griffen, E. Studley, Frank Russell, and Holledge. Other players who helped to make the team famous were: The Rev. A. P. Baines, Tommy Fitchie, William Fitchie, E. E. Cretchley, G. Neil, Rainbird, Jimmy Stone, Ossie Stone, Seppy and Charles Mann, Joe Landells, Ben Bullock, R. C. Steven, Bob Simpson, and Art Coppin. It has been said that the West Norwood F.C. was the first football club in the country to become a limited company. One of the club's officials was Baron Frederick W. von Reiffenstien. The club continued after the war of 1914–18, but not with its former glory, and with no ground available near Norwood it failed for lack of support. In addition to this senior football club, West Norwood has had many good junior clubs. Leigham United F.C. ran for many years. Then in the 1920's there was Silverdale, the fine team run by the West Norwood Brotherhood, and its rival club, Auckland United. Then came the Ivy Football Club, of which I was a founder-member, which changed its name later to Norwood F.C., and won many championships of the Dulwich and Streatham Leagues. A fine team was also run by Christ Church, Gipsy Hill.

Cricket does not seem to have played quite the same part in local sport as football. I think the absence of suitable grounds for cricket in Norwood, and the growing popularity of tennis, account for the decline of cricket in recent years. Many years ago the Grecian Cricket Club, under the patronage of "Dick" Fry, had its ground in Crown Lane, and included among its players—Mr. W. W. Gill, W. Masters, T. M. Richards, T. E. Wheeler, Shrimpton, and W. Hooten. Other cricket clubs were the Wasps and Thornlaw C.C.

Having paused to consider sport, let us return to York Hill again. The railway which passes under the railway bridge, known as West Norwood junction has recently been relaid with one of the first all-cast crossings to be installed on the Southern section.

Knollys Road, by the railway bridge, contains two houses worthy of mention. What is the mystery behind No. 156, the house which has stood empty and derelict for so many years? No one seems to know who owns it, and there it stands, weather-beaten and dilapidated, surrounded by dense trees and undergrowth. The other house is an imposing residence called Thurlow Towers, a fine red brick house of comparatively recent times, once the residence of Mr. Michael Pope, F.S.A. Built into the ornamental garden wall just inside the front gate were some large carved blocks of stone which seemed to have been part of a carved stone frieze. For many years they stood derelict on a piece of waste ground at the corner of Crown Lane and Knight's Hill until they were taken to Thurlow Towers. They have now been taken away again.

From Knollys Road we must return to Norwood Road. I have spoken of the houses from York Hill to the one which was pulled down to make way for the Regal Cinema. Now we come to another little backwater of Norwood, Thomas Place, now called Waylett Place after the actress Harriet Waylett (Kate Carney) who is buried in Norwood Cemetery. Some of the little cottages here have only two rooms on the ground floor and but one room above. Tradesmen connected with the shops between the Regal Cinema and the present post office were—Woodgate, cabinet maker; Griggs, decorator; Bryder (afterwards Good Bros.), greengrocer; Mrs. Baines, toy bazaar; Mrs. Fairweather, music; W. Sheard, butcher; and Dixon, stationer. From Waylett Place to Lansdowne Hill were Cartwright, photographer; Carlin, corn merchant; Valler, hairdresser; Laflin, tailor; and Dulley (now Seamans) baker. Carlin's shop was built on the front of an old house, built so I have been told from stone taken from the old London Bridge. On the right side of Lansdowne Hill are firstly two shops, once occupied by Mr. Lamont, hairdresser, and Cuddon, builder. Then came little Sydenham Terrace (Lansdowne Hill was once Sydenham Grove and York Hill was Dulwich Grove) with its one or two little cottages and Mr. Langton's forge.

Between Sydenham Terrace and the house next to it up the hill, by the side of a small piece of ground on which Mr. R. Gray, the stonemason, used to display memorial stones, you can still see some of the old tramway rails leading in to the premises which were once the depot and stables of the old horse-drawn trams of the South London Tramway Company. These old horse-drawn trams used to run from the cemetery to Coldharbour Lane, then left to Stockwell or right to Camberwell Green. The service was slow and the fares dear. In those days there was no conductor to collect fares; the passengers dropped their pence into a box behind the driver, and he supplied the change if needed. I don't think these trams ever paid a dividend. They were replaced by the present electric trams about the year 1908, and these trams will in their turn disappear. A horse bus service worked about every half an hour from the "Thurlow Arms" to Brixton, over Tulse Hill. The fare was sixpence. These buses were run by Messrs. Ball Bros.

Some of Norwood's original old houses stood on the right-hand side of Lansdowne Hill below the railway bridge. I will mention these later in connection with the Convent. The railway bridge was partly rebuilt in 1939, and the embankment has given a lot of trouble at this spot for some years. Just over the bridge on the left is the somewhat odd row of houses called Mount Villas. The first one or two houses on the left side of Lansdowne Hill were pulled down when Woolworth's store was erected. Where Lansdowne Hall now stands was a private residence approached by a drive; it was called Castle House.

We have already seen how the Rev. Fuller Gooch, after 13 years as Pastor of Chatsworth Road Baptist Church, resigned so as to be free of denominational ties. Mr. Gooch was persuaded to remain in Norwood and to initiate a Church on a strictly unsectarian basis. On the 8th May, 1892, the first service of the new church took place in the old Public Hall. Then a freehold piece of ground was secured in Lansdowne Hill at a cost of £900, and a corrugated-iron hall to seat 900 persons was erected at a cost of £1,400. The first service in this hall was held on 12th April, 1893. In 1895 the building was enlarged, and in 1897 additional land was secured and a permanent lecture hall for Y.M.C.A. and other services erected. In 1906 steps were taken to build a permanent building in place of the iron hall, which I believe was afterwards re-erected at Clacton-on-Sea. The foundation stone of the new building was laid by Lord Kinnaird on the 7th July, 1906, and the building was opened for public worship on the 7th March, 1907. The total cost was £6,200. Mr. Gooch carried on a good work here for upwards of 30 years until his death at the age of 85. His son, Mr. H. Martyn Gooch, is the secretary of the World's Evangelical Alliance. Lansdowne Hall was burnt out during an air raid in 1944. Services were then held in the smaller hall.

On the corner of Canterbury Grove and Lansdowne Hill was the original office of "Ye Olde Norwood Presse" as it was called. Messrs. Truslove and Bray Ltd. the proprietors, afterwards took larger premises in Nettlefold Place. The "Norwood Press" was first published as a monthly in May 1882. It later became a weekly, and was distributed free around the neighbourhood. For over 60 years it has faithfully recorded all the happenings in the neighbourhood, and copies of it are sent all over the globe each week to old "Norwegians" now exiled to other parts. Some of the original advertisers are still advertising in its pages. Much space has always been given to the social and religious activities in Norwood, and no space at all to the sort of news such a one finds in the sensational Sunday papers. Its Reader's Column has its regular contributors. The Editor for over fifty years was the late Mr. H. G. Warr, who was succeeded by Mr. Wm. C. Lockwood.

There are some old Norwood houses both above and below the footbridge (known locally as the "Wooden Bridge") in Canterbury Grove, where is the modern factory of Tannoy Ltd., the well-known manufacturers of sound-amplifying equipment. Founded by Mr. Guy R. Fountain, this firm began in small premises in Dalton Street, one of its first public address systems being installed at the Ideal Homes Exhibition at Olympia.

At the corner of Lansdowne Hill and Norwood Road stood a tall rather ugly house, lying back with railings in front of it. It was occupied by Mr. Jackson, a stonemason, whose son occupied the same premises as a photographer. The front garden of the house was then covered with the shop premises of Wright Bros., the drapers. Woolworth's store now stands on the site. Next, towards Bloom Grove, were three small old-fashioned shops: Weare, harness maker; Martin, tobacconist; and Valler, hairdresser. Next to these shops was Mr. James's Castle Nursery, named after the house in Lansdowne Hill. Then Piper's, monumental masons, with the yard at the side. This business was later The Art Memorial Company, proprietor, Mr. Edwards. At the corner of Bloom Grove stood Mr. Good (afterwards Folletts), bakers, with Mr. Thorn, grocer and verger of St. Luke's Church. Bloom Grove, one of Norwood's many quiet cul-de-sacs, in the shape of a letter Y, contains some large houses around a triangular grass plot bordered with trees. A small beer shop called "Ivy House" used to stand at the corner of Bloom Grove and Knight's Hill.

So we have come back to the fountain, having completed our tour of the Norwood Road district, and from this point our journey will take us along Norwood High Street. When St. Luke's Church was built in 1825, Norwood High Street and Elder Road were both called Elderhole Road after a large coppice of trees called the Great Elderhole Coppice which covered Elder Road from Norwood Park to Gipsy Road school. On a map of Norwood which I have, dated 1858, the road is marked as Elder Road from St. Luke's Church to Central Hill. Somewhere about 1870 when it was the principal shopping centre of the neighbourhood the lower half of the road became High Street, Lower Norwood. There can be no doubt that the railway bridge across the High Street, being too low for buses to pass under and too narrow for tram lines, has cramped the development of Norwood High Street into a main shopping centre of any consequence.

Chapter 6
Norwood High Street

Starting from Norwood Road, the first four houses in Norwood High Street, between the two cemetery gates, were obviously built at the same time as St. Luke's Church, for they are adorned with the same Grecian pediments as the church. The first house, next to the cemetery, was Osborne Lodge, where lived a solicitor, Mr. Honey, and was afterwards Yeatman's the stonemasons. Next door, Messrs. Clayton and Hopkins carried on a carpet beating and chimney sweeping business for many years. In front of the next house stood the greengrocery stall of Mrs. Williams, while the last of the four was once occupied by Mr. Bolingbroke, a stonemason. These houses were almost totally destroyed by a flying bomb in 1944. Past the High Street gate of the cemetery we come to the shop where Mr. Charles Butler had a tool-grinding business. Mr. Butler's brother Jack was a famous walking champion, and his brother Alfred carried on a coachbuilder's business. Next is Madame Carless, drapery. In one of the little houses that comes next lives Mr. Alfred Heath, the highly-respected carman and contractor. The shop at the corner of Dunbar Street was once Mr. Crookers', boot repairer, later Mrs. Johnson's, wardrobe dealer. In Dunbar Street, or Elm Grove, as it then was, stood a large house known as Elm Grove Academy, conducted by a Mr. Simpson. A few yards down on the right-hand side stands Bethel Chapel, built by my great-grandfather in 1868. I have his notebook still, recording the amounts paid to workmen, cost of bricks, hire of scaffolding, etc.

His notebook says: "Chappell cost 355.16.10."
On the other side of the page:

"Collection (probably at opening)	£26. 2. 0½
Tea	2. 3. 7
Sunday collection	3. 14. 0
	31. 19. 7½
Cash received from loan and Gifts	302. 15.11½
Do.	6. 10. 0¾
	£341. 5. 7¾
Balance due to builder	£14. 11. 2½"

My great-grandfather was one of the first deacons of this church, and a list of pew sittings is also in the notebook. Its first and only pastor was the Rev. M. Silvester, who collapsed and died in the pulpit one Sunday morning shortly after announcing his text, which was "Rejoice in the Lord, again I say rejoice." There is a memorial tablet to his memory in the church and also one to the memory of my great-grandfather and to Mr. Read, another deacon. In 1938 the chapel was taken over by the London City Mission, who transferred their cause from Elim Hall. The building was then entirely redecorated and modernised under the direction of the missionary, Mr. J. Atwell. My brother, the Rev. Leonard C. Wilson, a great-grandson of a founder, preached the first sermon from the text: "The Glory of this latter house shall be greater than of the former." In the early days of the chapel, conventions were held there from time to time. My grandfather told me that on these occasions the visiting ministers would come to my great-grandfather's to dinner, and after dinner would sit on the hearthrug in front of the fire smoking church-warden pipes which my grandfather had been sent to purchase the day before at Mr. Putley's shop opposite. One of these visiting ministers was the Rev. James Pert of Flimwell near Hastings, whose daughter married my grandfather.

A few yards past the Chapel was the first Salvation Army Barracks in Norwood in a yard now occupied by Mr. Heath. Mention of the yard brings to my mind that queer old character known as "Norwood Joe" who used to sleep in a loft there.

In the wall at the side of the corner shop that was Mrs. Johnson's can be seen a stone tablet which bears this inscription: "Model Cottages, Elm Grove". The cottages of Dunbar Street and Wood Street (now Dunbar Place) are characteristic of most of the cottage property first built in Lower Norwood.

At the corner of Dunbar Street and Wood Street stood the curiously named public house, "The No. 1". This little public house was popular as it was off the beaten track, so to speak. It was closed under the Redundancy Act in June, 1935. "Are we to part like this, Bill?" was sung by its old customers as its doors closed for the last time as a tribute to Mr. William Hartwell, who ministered to the thirst of his neighbours there for 28 years. Another little public house closed under the Redundancy Act was "The Castle" which stood at the corner of Dunbar Street and Norwood High Street. It is now a coffee shop, but you can still see the castle worked into the design of the frosted glass panel of its front door. This glass panel has survived even though a bomb fell right outside in 1940. The local name for this public house was the "Roaring Donkey" because of the fights that took place there, especially on Saturday nights.

From "The Castle" to the Roman Catholic Church the shops call to mind: Mr. Parsons, greengrocery; Mr. Leech, second-hand furniture; a yard with stabling and workshops with a small shop at the entrance, once Mr. Gant, zinc-worker. Then was Binstead (later Sanders), grocer; Mr. Thomas Knowlden, butcher, and Mr. Scott, boot repairer. Then came a large double-fronted house called "Violet Bank" once the residence of the Bowyer family, the well-known builders. The large front garden of the house was selected for the erection of St. Matthew's Roman Catholic Church, which was certified as a place of public worship in December 1905. This was largely due to the generosity of Miss Frances Elizabeth Ellis. The old house remained behind the church as the presbytery, but was pulled down in 1935 to make room for a much-needed extension to the church. A new house, incorporating a parish hall, was built for the priest in the back garden of the old house. An old well over forty feet deep was discovered during the building. The much respected Rev. Father Joseph Galea, D.D., was priest-in-charge for thirty seven years. A native of Malta, Father Galea did a good work in West Norwood. He was an artist of no mean repute, and the large painting of the Crucifixion above the altar was his work. It must have been a severe blow to him when the newly-enlarged church was partly demolished by a bomb in November, 1940. He died suddenly just before the morning service on Sunday, 1st of February, 1942, and was succeeded by the Rev. Father Alfred J. Cole.

The bomb which damaged the church also demolished the shop next door which was for many years Mr. Hobday's, jeweller. The Norwood Drug Store comes next, and the shop at the corner of Auckland Hill, once kept by Mr. George Kemp, grocer. On or near the site of the present Cranfield Villas stood a house similar to "Violet Bank." The ground here must have been filled in a great deal to make the road, for at the end of Cranfield Villas there is a considerable drop behind the wall across the end of the road down into the back gardens of Wood Street. The builder's premises at the corner of Cranfield Villas and Auckland Hill was the original Co-operative Store in West Norwood.

To return to the other side of High Street. Next to St. Luke's Church stood the original Norwood Fire Station, now the Parish Hall. Before this fire station was built in 1881 the nearest fire station was on the Crystal Palace Parade. I remember my grandfather telling me that in the late 1860's his workshop caught fire, and he rode on horseback to the Crystal Palace to fetch the fire engine. In the meantime the workshop burned to the ground. When I was a small boy I was allowed to stay up until 9 o'clock on Saturday night if I was good so that I could go down to the fire station in High Street to see the horse-drawn fire engines turn out for their weekly practice run. What a thrill it was! At 9 o'clock the bells would ring, firemen would slide down the brass pole, rush the horses from the stables, harness them to the engine, and when all was ready the driver would pull the rope that mysteriously opened the doors, and away they would gallop. First the escape with its ladder swaying, then the engine with smoke coming from its chimney, and with much jingling of harness bells they would gallop as far as the corner of Chapel Road and back. Later as a schoolboy, my bosom friend was Arthur Henn, son of the superintendent of the fire station, and I was then able to add to my earlier thrills. For with my friend I was able to visit the stables, climb the watch-tower, and also to clamber up the ladder of the spare escape which stood in the yard at the side. Mr. Henn succeeded

Mr. Dane, the first superintendent, who went to live at Deal on retiring, and lived to the ripe old age of 94. While at Norwood fire station Mr. Dane instituted a novel way of announcing the result of the annual Varsity Boat Race. As soon as the result came through either a light or dark blue flag was run up to the top of the flag mast on top of the watch-tower.

In 1917, after the fire station had been moved to a larger and more modern building in Norwood Road, the old station was purchased by the council of St. Luke's Church and was converted into a parish hall. In 1927, this hall was enlarged, and the whole of the ground floor was rebuilt, taking in the old yard at the back and side. In this yard, the West Norwood ambulance was kept. This motor vehicle was purchased and maintained by local subscribers, but it was not a very successful venture, and did not last for many years. The absence of a regular driver was a great drawback; it was driven by many volunteer drivers and its maintenance was also a great problem. The ambulance staff were members of the St. John Ambulance Brigade, Mr. Alfred Vincent being the leader. From the fire station to Hannen Road the shops were occupied by first an Irishman named O'Connor, butcher, which afterwards became Mr. Harry Corline's, newsagent. Then was Stoneham's, ham and beef stores; then the Eclipse, a high class confectionery store, kept by that charming old couple, Mr. and Mrs. Larcombe. Mr. Walker's off-licence stood at the corner of Hannen Road.

I will speak of Hannen Road and Auckland Hill later, so we will now pass under the railway bridge and review first the East, or Auckland Hill side of the High Street to Gipsy Road corner, and then the other side to Chapel Road. Almost beside the railway bridge at the corner of Pilgrim Hill and High Street you can still see one of Lower Norwood's old shops, with its bow-fronted windows and their many panes of glass. Nowadays one thinks of the High Street as a road of shops, but originally there were only two rows of shops in the whole street. One adjoining the "Hope" public house consisted of about seven shops, the other row running from Chapel Road corner to the present Rothschild Street corner. The little bow-fronted shop was first occupied by a cornchandler, Mr. Lenny, and afterwards by Mr. George Tomlinson, a man greatly esteemed. Mr. Tomlinson was a staunch Wesleyan, and on Saturday nights one of his vans was placed on a piece of waste ground at the corner of Ernest Street and open-air meetings were conducted from it on Sundays. Messrs. H. Day & Sons afterwards took this little shop, and built the furniture store on the back and side of it. The "Hope" tavern is one of the oldest licensed premises in Norwood. Mr. James Keniston was landlord for a great many years as has likewise been the present landlord, Mr. Ernest Smith. Names associated with the row of shops adjoining are: Mrs. Smith, draper, afterwards Mr. Alfred Garey, second-hand furniture. Then Mr. Price, harness-maker, Mr. Chelmick, butcher, had two shops; then R. & J. Dick's boot shop; Mrs. Lawrence, afterwards Mrs. Oborn, confectioner, and Southwell, afterwards Bashford, baker. From here to the corner of Gipsy Road were small houses and cottages with front gardens. Some of the houses remain in their original condition, the Dove family having occupied some of them for generations. But most of the original cottages have now had shops built on their front gardens. Next to the houses occupied by the Dove family is the cornchandler's store of Mr. Tring, once occupied by a Mr. Crutcher. He also supplied the horse brakes for local outings. Then came Mr. Edwin Garey's greengrocer's shop, and Lower Norwood's principal draper Mr. W. H. Starke. Next door was the High Street Post Office, then Mr. Eli Bennet, off-licence. Mr. Bennet always wore in the shop a very ornamental smoking cap complete with tassel. Mr. W. Tatnell, grocer, came next, and at the corner of Waring Street Mr. Alfred Brice first opened his pawnbroking business.

Behind all this property from the "Hope" to this corner is a triangle of roads formed by East Street, East Place, and Change Alley. The latter is now called Dunkirk Street and East Street is now called Waring Street. The name is taken from a memorial tablet in St. Luke's Church to Samuel Waring, of Norwood, "Father of the Society for Promoting Christian Knowledge," (S.P.C.K.). At the corner where Dunkirk Street meets East Place there still stands a building which was once a cow-shed, part of Ayre's dairy. East Place runs along the side of the railway embankment with the arches of the viaduct at its commencement. These railway arches have been used for various purposes. I can remember the arch by the side of the High Street railway bridge behind Mr. Tomlinson's shop being opened as a small picture palace with a row of electric lights over the entrance. The small cottages in East Place were, I believe, originally built for the workmen engaged on the railway. At the commencement of these cottages was a small public house, the "Fox and Hounds", always referred to locally as the "Old Top Hat" because someone had once climbed to the top of its swinging signpost and placed a top hat on it. This hat remained there for so long that it gave the public house its nickname. Behind the "Fox and Hounds" was a large room where the local bird fanciers would gather on a Sunday morning. I have seen an old handbill advertising a "Smoking concert to be held at the Fox and Hounds, East Place, for the benefit of a Mr. . . ., who, owing to the death of his wife, has been left entirely without support." This little out-of-the-way public house was closed under the Redundancy Act and was demolished together with all the other little cottages in East Street and East Place under the L.C.C.'s clearance scheme in 1937-8, thereby sadly uprooting many families who had lived there for generations and who had cultivated the strip of land beside the railway embankment, by which the River Effra once flowed, as very well-kept allotment gardens. At the corner of Waring Street and Norwood High Street was Mr. W. Wootton, greengrocer, then came Mr. Beale, toy shop, now Mr. Beer, boot-repairer, and then the two shops which are of particular interest to me.

It was in 1830 that my great-great-grandfather first came to these premises in Norwood. The original lease is still in existence between James Corner, builder, and James Benson Wilson, yeoman, dated March 1830, and the premises are described in the lease as being on the east side of Elderhole Road, Lower Norwood, Surrey. The premises were then just a four-roomed cottage with a small scullery at the back. Here my ancestor began his business of cabinet-maker, upholsterer, and undertaker. When he retired he went to live in a house off Chapel Road where Woodcote Place now stands, and the business was carried on by his son, my great-grandfather, who built Bethel Chapel. My great-grandfather also took the cottage next door, and built shop fronts on the front gardens of both of them. By this time the population had grown, his duties as an undertaker were more numerous, so one of the two shops was used for this purpose, and the other for the cabinet-making. After his death both businesses were carried on by my grandfather, but on his retirement the furniture, cabinet-making, and the building sides of the business were all discontinued, and only the undertaker's business was carried on by my father and now by myself. So that five generations of J. B. Wilsons have lived and conducted business in these same premises.

Of the funerals and funeral customs of the old days I could almost write a separate book. I have all the books of the business right back to 1840, and in the early days the account of each funeral took up a whole foolscap page. They include such items as payment of tolls, hire of mutes, hire of velvet pall, hatbands and gloves for gentlemen, cloaks and gloves for ladies, and, at the end, refreshments for men. Mutes, there were usually two, were men dressed in black, with their top hats adorned by black silk hatbands like black silk scarves tied round the hat with the ends hanging down at the back. They wore black silk sashes over their shoulders, while in their hands they held mutes' poles, shaped like polo sticks and draped with black crepe. I have two of these poles still. These two men would stand at the front door of the house for an hour before the funeral, and would walk in front of the cortege to the cemetery. In those early days nearly all the local funerals to St. Luke's churchyard or Norwood cemetery were walking funerals. The coffin was carried, often by relays of men, sometimes from as far as Woodland Road, the mourners walking behind. The first horse-drawn hearses were like a large box on wheels (glass-sided hearses came later). The sides were draped with black velvet, and huge black plumes of feathers were placed on top of it. The horses also had these black plumes on their heads and velvet cloth over their backs, two, four or even six horses being used. If six were used a postillion in a black velvet jacket rode on the leading near-side horse. The bearers who walked beside the hearse carried short oak staffs with brass ends called truncheons, while beside each carriage walked a "page" who carried a "wand" like the wand of office carried by churchwardens. Its purpose was to assist him to keep the crowd back from the carriage doors. Coffins in the early days were always covered with black cloth studded with many rows of brass nails in various panels and patterns. All the pomp and show has now disappeared with all the deep mourning clothes that went with it.

Next to my grandfather's shop was a grocer's shop kept by Mr. Raven; afterwards it was Mr. Priest, greengrocer (later Wiles). Then came Mr. Joseph Willmot, picture-frame maker. I can always tell a picture-frame made by Mr. Willmot, as he, being left-handed, always put his nails in the frame at the opposite side to anyone else. Then came Armstrong & Southby, drapers; Rowland Ellis, grocery store; Redknaps, gent's outfitter; and Rowland Ellis's provision stores, now Rasmers. The passage beside this shop led to Mr. Wheeler's forge, now a builder's workshop. The quaint little butcher's shop of Mr. Crouch was once Mr. Griffiths, and at the back of it is the slaughter-house, still used for slaughtering. There were gates at the top of the passage beside the shop which could be closed to prevent the cattle from escaping from the yard. Next door to the butcher's shop is the only one of the original four-roomed cottages in its original condition, with its front garden. This was the residence for many years of Mr. Bastin the builder. Mr. Coe, boot repairer, had the next shop; then Mr. Candy, second-hand furniture; Rowland Ellis's oil and colour store; and at the corner of Windsor Road (now Grove) was Mr. E. Thewless, greengrocer.

Windsor Road was a quiet little backwater. On the left-hand side behind Mr. Thewless' shop stood a small whitewashed cottage (one-storied). Next door to it was a small chapel, first used as a Methodist Chapel in 1838. It then became Primitive Methodist, and finally ceased to be a place of worship in 1901. It was then used by Mr. C. Barber as a carpenter's workshop. The building is still standing and is now part of the Advance Laundry premises. Where this laundry now stands was Mr. Anstey's nursery, with a lovely row of poplars along the Windsor Road frontage. On the right-hand side of Windsor Road from High Street was first a small row of two-storied cottages, then at the corner of a short cul-de-sac was the Norwood Rifle Range. From this short turning to the end of Windsor Road are several large residences, the first of which, at the corner, was called Canton Villa. This was used by the West Norwood Brotherhood as its institute before the present buildings on Knight's Hill were opened. In the turning beside Canton Villa there were some stables belonging to the houses.

The four shops in High Street from the corner of Windsor Grove were occupied by Mr. Walker, toy shop; later Mr. Jones, boot-repairer, then Mr. Kettley, draper; Mr. W. Hammond, hot water and gas fitter, and Mr. Creese, confectioner. In the window of Mr. Hammond's shop the first incandescent mantle was demonstrated, and caused quite a sensation, the pavement being filled with admiring spectators. Though this may seem strange now, it can be readily understood when we remember that up to that time the general lighting was fish-tail for

gas and Argand burners for paraffin lamps. The first prices were, mantles 1/3d, burners, 3/6d. Next to the shops stand four charming little cottages facing Rothschild Street. Built over 120 years ago I have been told that they were a copy of some almhouses somewhere in London but that I have not been able to confirm. From these cottages to Gipsy Road there was only a piece of waste ground until the houses called Ash Villas were built, and then the four shops to the corner. The corner shop was opened by a French lady chemist named Madame Eugenie, and next door was the stationery shop of Mr. Mowell, now Mr. Lake's.

Now to return to the railway bridge to follow the west side of High Street. The first turning is Cotswold Street, once called Gloucester Street, the top half of which belongs to the railway company, and is closed every Good Friday to preserve the company's rights. At the corner stands the "Gipsy Queen" public house. The row of shops which adjoined it in Cotswold Street have now been converted into dwelling-houses. The shops were once occupied by—Mrs. Chalklin, china and glass; Mr. C. J. Horne, second-hand furniture; C. Broomfield, boot repairer; Mrs. Oborn, dining rooms; Austin, pawnbroker; and Horgan, fried fish shop (at the corner of Beadman Street), Mr. Cornwall's printing works a little higher up is also an old established business. Also in Cotswold Street were the Norwood Charity Office and the original West Norwood Sorting Office. The shops in High Street from the "Gipsy Queen" to Langmead Street have also been converted into dwelling houses. These premises remind us of Frake, chemist; Michie, watch repairer; Traye, tailor; Garey, greengrocer; Hatton, butcher; and Allen, grocer.

Mr. Langmead, who built Langmead Square, intended them to be high-class dwellings, but as our American friends would say they "failed to make the grade", and were let out as tenements. The left-hand side of Langmead Square where Elim Hall stands was an unfenced piece of waste ground, and was often used by a travelling auctioneer called Old Rowley. His visits, usually on a Saturday, would cause some fun. He would arrive in a caravan with a large tailboard. From this tailboard he would extend a long plank with its other end resting on an up-turned barrel. A clown would run up and down this plank offering the goods for sale to the large crowd which gathered, with many witty remarks and droll stories. To attract custom Old Rowley would hold competitions, giving prizes for various things. One time it would be for the finest cat in the neighbourhood. Mr. H. J. Moyes told me that he has a silver cup presented by Old Rowley to his mother, which Mr. Moyes won as the fattest baby in Norwood. Another time a race between boys was organised; the first boy to eat a hot treacle dumpling suspended by a string was given a prize. All this of course to attract customers to his business of selling goods by auction.

Elim Hall was built by the London City Mission. Mr. Veryard was the well liked missionary there for many years. At the other corner of Langmead Street and High Street was Mr. Fellingham, baker. Then came Mr. Paine, hairdresser, and Mr. Bryant, tailor. Next to the contractor's yard (which was Mr. Clarkson's for many years) stands the quaint little old house, now no. 44. This house with its bow-fronted window must be one of the oldest in the neighbourhood. It was occupied by a Mrs. Frowde and later by R. Booth, second-hand dealer, who used the wooden shed at the left hand side of it for displaying his goods. The big irregular old cobble-stones in the yard at the side of the house are also of very early date. The shops from here to the corner of Ernest Avenue bring to mind the names of—Keener, later Cripps, cornchandler; Mr. Roberts, later Mr. Jarvis, grocer; Mr. Mummery, fishmonger; Mr. A. L. Brice, pawnbroker (still there); Pell, ironmonger; also Mr. Venturi, who was always called Ice Cream Jack. He used to stand with his ice-cream barrow outside the "Thurlow Arms". Then was Smart, later Hawes, now Collingwood, butcher. At the corner of Ernest Avenue was a rough space on which Mr. Southby built the large premises which is now a Co-operative store, and transferred his draper's business there from the small shop on the other side of the road. It is strange that Mr. Southby's business did not flourish in these larger premises as it did in the smaller one. It has happened on several occasions that a flourishing small business has for no apparent reason ceased to flourish when larger premises have been taken. The "importance of being Ernest" was stressed when the L.C.C. proposed to change the name of Ernest Street to Shrubsall Road, the residents protesting that it would be a difficult name to say even when sober; and in the most unlikely event of any of them being otherwise how could they hope to give their home address. So Ernest Street became Ernest Avenue instead of Shrubsall Road. At first it had no outlet to Knight's Hill. It was a cul-de-sac only a few yards long until 1858 when it was further extended, but it was not until about 40 years ago that Mr. James's nursery that blocked the Knight's Hill end of it was pulled down and the road was opened through to Knight's Hill. Entering Ernest Street from High Street we find on the right-hand side first an archway leading to some stabling where was once a large slaughter-house to which flocks of sheep were often driven in my grandfather's day. Next to this archway lived Mr. Chamberlain, cab proprietor. A little further on is another archway which led to premises used for carpet-beating and stables by my grandfather. Yet another little opening further down leads to Hope Cottage, a little dwelling once occupied by Mr. Tullet, signalman at West Norwood station. The row of cottages named Khyber Cottages completes that side of the street.

On the left-hand side from High Street the first house was occupied by Mr. Martin, the sweep, for many years, and next to this a small opening one side of which is called Ernest Place and the other side Charlotte Place. The next three houses all had tradesmen's boards attached to them when they were occupied by Mr. Beeson, umbrella-maker; Mr. Staples, cab proprietor (now Mr. Weaver, plumber) and Mr. Cuddon, decorator. Then we come to a business that has been established for a hundred years, the Halstead Laundry. Next to this is yet another little passage-way in this street of many backwaters. It led to some cottages, demolished in 1937, called Eaton Cottages. Yet another opening led to a house well back from the road, once occupied by Mr. Ward, a builder.

At the corner of Ernest Street and High Street opposite the Co-operative stores, stood the British Workman dining-rooms. Originally built for a public house it failed to get a licence owing to the large number of public houses already in existence nearby. It was opened as a coffee tavern by Mr. G. A. Green who was born on June 11th 1836, died in May 1938 a few days short of his 102nd birthday. He was much respected, and in hard winters would make soup to give to poor people. On Sunday he would turn his shop into a place of worship, and never tired of telling how he was converted at Park Street Chapel under the influence of the Rev. C. H. Spurgeon. Over his shop doorway he erected a stone tablet with the following inscription:

"If I'm alive, I'm up at five,
If you but give a call,
I'll have a cup of coffee hot,
I know will please you all."

The rooms above the shop were used for slate clubs, and the basement for band practice. These dining-rooms were later run by Mr. Bailey.

The next-door shop was Mrs. Booth's, wardrobe dealer; and then a hairdresser's, Mr. Long. This shop was later a draper's kept by the Misses Hutchings. The piece of ground on which the next four shops were built was first considered by the Board of Works for the erection of the fire station, but it was decided to build it further down the street. Between these shops and the "King's Head" stood two houses; one, now a petrol station, belonged to Mr. Simpson a contractor.

The old "King's Head" was the centre of life and gaiety in the High Street. The old building stood further back from the road than the present one, with a forecourt, similar to the present "Thurlow Arms". On Saturday evenings there was usually a local band playing in front of the "King's Head", and also one or two stalls. A local man, Mr. Sam Ayres, had a small stall on which he made toffee. This toffee was cut up into different-sized pieces which were placed round a spinning jenny. Children paid a penny, spun the jenny, and where the pointer stopped that was their piece of toffee. At the right-hand side of the old bulding was a doorway leading to a large building at the back, used by travelling theatrical companies, who produced thrilling dramas such as *Sweeney Todd*, *East Lynne*, etc. At the left-hand side of the "King's Head" was a gateway leading into pleasure gardens called the Tivoli Gardens. One of the attractions of the gardens was a small monkey-house; another was a maze. The grounds were used for playing cricket, quoits, and skittles. A well-known landlord of the old "King's Head" was

Mr. Drouet, nicknamed Doctor Drouet. This because he always knew a remedy for all ills. For instance anyone asking for a drop of rum for a cold would be told "You don't want rum, take this home and try it." "This" being some remedy of his own. It is difficult to draw in words a picture of the old "King's Head" as it used to be, with the crowd, the cries of traders, the flaring jets on the stalls, the music of the band, etc. Saturday night was Saturday night then with the shops open until midnight. They had to be for those were the days when wages were often paid in the pubic houses.

Next to the "King's Head" was Mr. Pyett's timber yard, at the side of which was a contractor's yard. Then we come to yet another of those little public houses long since closed, the "Forester's Arms", which stood facing Windsor Grove. The landlord of this public house would not allow women to enter it, and there was a spinning jènny on the ceiling which was a popular way of deciding who should pay for the drinks. Almost next door was a dingy, unattractive little shop where Mr. Putley dealt in tops, whistles, blacking, and bundles of wood and coal in frugal portions for the poorer people. I have mentioned this shop before in connection with the long clay churchwarden pipes. Over the shop, with a separate entrance and staircase, was a room used by the Plymouth Brethren for their services. Over the doorway were the words "Cave of Abdullam." The shop is now a newsagent's once owned by Mr. Tom Angus. The other shops in this row to the corner of Rothschild Street were: Bremner, later Wright, baker; and Mr. Parrett, grocer. Where Rothschild Street is now stood a private house first called Elder Cottage, but its last occupant, Mr. Gardiner, changed the name to King's Langley because he came from that place. From Rothschild Street to Chapel Road stood the row of shops called Castle Terrace, one of High Street's two original rows of shops. The shop at the corner of Rothschild Street is modern, having been build by Mr. Allman who transferred his gentleman's outfitter's business from smaller premises in High Street. Traders whose names are connected with Castle Terrace are: A. Thompson, fishmonger; Woolway, boots and shoes; Cowes, draper; Coomber, later Colman, hairdresser; Bristow, builder; Casswell, butcher; Andrews, newsagent; H. Thompson, pork butcher; Burr, corn chandler; Beeson, music; Deacon, watchmaker; Poole, oil and colour; and Ford, general draper. Mr. Alfred Thompson, a grand old gentleman, will be remembered as Norwood's Registrar of Births and Deaths.

Chapter 7
Chapel Road

Chapel Road, once called Gypsey House Road, is one of the oldest in Norwood. Like Ernest Avenue, it has several little backwaters and is full of interest, having changed little during the past 60 years. Starting from High Street and taking the left-hand side first, we come to three of the original Norwood Cottages. An old lady, Miss Gameson, kept the first as a lollipop shop, and did a good trade with the schoolboys. Her stock-in-trade included lollipops, sugar-sticks, Jumbo chains made of liquorice, bull's-eyes, peppermints, acid drops, and rainbow balls which changed colour as they were sucked. The third cottage was occupied by Mr. Charles Barber, the builder. The cottages drew water from a well in their back gardens. A well next door to a burial ground does not strike me as being particularly healthy. For these cottages are next door to the Congregational Chapel which has a small burial ground at the back. The gravestones have been moved back against the walls for many years. Among the graves are those of two workmen killed in a scaffolding accident during the erection of the Crystal Palace.

The Congregational Chapel is the oldest Nonconformist church in the neighbourhood. The gates and railings in the front are, I believe, hand wrought. The date of opening in June 1820 (five years before St. Luke's Church was opened) could be seen on an old iron lamp-standard at the back of the church. Allen's *History of Lambeth* (1825) describes it as a "neat Chapel in Norwood for Independents, with no galleries or organ and capable of holding about 600." (p. 434) Galleries were added later. Mr. J. Corbett Anderson in his book *Upper, West and South Norwood* on page 14 says:

"Although an earlier chapel appears to have once stood near the site, the oldest nonconformist place of worship now existing in West Norwood is situated in a road to which it has given the name Chapel Road. The freehold on which it stands was presented by that Mr. Salter from whom Salter's Hill derives its name."

The *History of Lambeth* says—

"Schools were attached 1824 conducted on British and Foreign school system. 250 of both sexes are educated."

These Nonconformist day schoolrooms consisted of a room at the back for the girls, one on the right of the church for infants, and one on the left for the boys. Mr. Charles Wilson was headmaster for many years, and became the first headmaster at Gipsy Road School when the Board Schools were established. In its palmy days the Congregational Church was a very fashionable church, and carriages were to be seen in a double line along the road waiting for the well-to-do people from all over the district attending the services on Sundays. Well-known ministers of the church have been: the Rev. Benjamin Kent, and the Rev. Dr. McCann, both of whom were noted preachers who drew large crowds. Then came the Rev. Samuel King, the first to wear a gown, a gift of the ladies of the church. He went to Westgate-on-Sea. The name of the Rev. Walter Baxendale will always be connected with the chapel. A great personality, he took part with great zest in the politics of the day. Among later ministers were the Rev. Hilton Smith, the Rev. A. Sloper, the Rev. M. Laverack and the Rev. A. C. Gravelle, now Nonconformist minister at Norwood Cemetery.

The house next to the Chapel at the corner of Curnick's Lane was the residence of Mr. Curnick, a stonemason. In the lane are several typical old Norwood cottages. Between the lane and the present Ladas Road (named after a Derby winner) stood a house known as Hollingbourne House Academy, a private school later known as Westwood's Academy. Then a gate leading to meadow land used by the Brewery opposite for grazing. Next to this stood the "Boat House" so called because it was built representing a boat. The house stood well back, and had a large garden with a small gate and a lodge near the pavement. Then a few old-fashioned shops to the corner of Woodcote Place, one of which was kept by Mr. Spargo, a florist, another by Mr. Bartley Wilson, later Mr. Wallis, a grocer's. Woodcote Place was originally a cul-de-sac, consisting of about a dozen semi-detached houses at its lower end. A row of small fir trees grew across the road just above them and blocked the highway. From Woodcote Place to Eden Road the shops and houses are still unaltered. The shop at the corner of Woodcote Place was Mr. Arnold's butcher's shop. Mr. Arnold was one of the old type of tradesmen, and wore a top hat while conducting his business. Mr. Smith, the chemist, was for many years at the corner of Eden Road. In the first house on the left in Eden Road lived an old coal merchant, Mr. Barker, who used to take his horse right through the house to its stable in his back garden every day. Just above his house was Mr. Ranger's wheelwright's shop, in the front of which lay a large circular flat stone used for stretching the iron tyres on cart-wheels. On the right-hand side is the Eden Road Day school of which we will speak when we come to the Wesleyan Church to which it belongs. From Eden Road to Knight's Hill the shops and houses have not altered.

On the other corner of Chapel Road and Knight's Hill stands the Norwood Technical Institute. Originally called The Lower Norwood Working Men's Institute it was presented by Mr. Arthur Anderson. He also gave the houses next to it on Knight's Hill called Stone Villas, and also the row of stone houses in Chapel Road called Maidstone Villas, to provide an income for the upkeep of the Institute. The following appeared in the *Illustrated London News* on the 10th March, 1860, entitled "The

Lower Norwood Working Men's Institute:"

"A building has been erected at the expense of Mr. Arthur Anderson of Lower Norwood, for the use of the Working Men's Institute of that district. It was inaugurated on Monday the 19th December last by 2 public meetings, one of them under the presidency of Sir Thomas Phillips, chairman of the Society of Arts, at 2 o'clock and the other in the evening when Mr. Anderson himself presided over a crowded and highly delighted assemblage. This Institute is an example of the success which may be confidently expected when sound plans are carefully carried out into action. It is a bona fide working men's institution, its affairs are under the general direction of working men and it is doing a vast amount of good in many different ways amongst the working men of Lower Norwood. The munificent aid rendered by Mr. A. Anderson, who has provided a building for the Institute entirely at his own cost, has enabled the committee to devote their energies to the development of their plans for the intellectual, social and moral amelioration of this neighbourhood. The building itself, from designs by Mr. Lamb, claims more than passing notice, as a really noble example of open-handed liberality. It is both admirably adapted for its purpose by the excellence and completeness of its arrangements and is also a felicitous instance of the applicability of Gothic architecture to existing requirements."

Compare this account with a modern newspaper report. The old-time journalists had a command of their own language.

The magazine of the Institute, the *House Flag*, gives the following account of the Institute's history:

"The history of the Institute is most conveniently considered in three episodes. During the first, from 1859 to 1895, it was under the control of Trustees and entirely supported by private funds and local effort. Then followed a period from 1895 to 1904 when it functioned as a branch of the Borough Polytechnic. In 1904 it was organised as one of the first separate maintained Institutes of the London County Council.

"During the first 35 years the building was used for a variety of purposes and its course was beset with difficulties which subsequently were found by the Trustees to be beyond their powers.

"Anderson, James Allen, and Thomas Hill constituted the first body of Trustees. They were permitted under certain conditions, to let the Hall and rooms in order to raise money for expenses limited to £50 in any one year. The annual value of the lease was £23, for a term of 80 years. The Lower Norwood Working Men's Institute was accommodated in the Institute where it prospered and rendered valuable service, under the stimulating influence of able persons such as the founder, Mr. Franks and the Rev. Benjamin Kent who were in a position to secure the co-operation of many educated men and women to assist them in their splendid voluntary effort.

"According to the scanty records available, about 80 per cent of the Institute's activities was devoted to the various functions of the Working Men's Institute. One can imagine that the lecture and debating courses were supplemented by classes in reading, writing and arithmetic. Flourishing drawing classes were conducted by Mr. Hale. The W.M.I. also organised social functions for its members and assisted in alleviating the sufferings due to extreme poverty which at times was all too prevalent in Norwood.

"There is no doubt that numerous dramatic and other societies found the Norwood Institute a satisfactory home. In these days it is difficult to realise that such enthusiasm could exist, when the stage was much smaller than at the present time, imperfect gas lighting the only means of illumination and inadequate open fires the only existing form of heating. Between 1890-4 the dramatic and other societies moved to the old Public Hall. In 1890 the building was sadly out of date. A cold draughty badly-lit Hall approached only by a narrow spiral staircase was certain to cause trouble. Nothing had been done in the past to modernise the Hall and later lack of money rendered improvements impossible. Sir Josiah Temple advanced a sum of £159 in a last effort to make the building attractive for letting. The closure of the building seemed imminent.

"This was however but the prelude to a notable change for the better. By 1895 evening classes had been inaugurated at Gipsy Road. The desire for education was evident. Sir Evan Spicer and others recognised that there was a chance of reviving the usefulness of the Norwood Institute.

"A public meeting was held on the 19th February, 1895, to consider the proposal for the establishment of a Branch Polytechnic in the Institute. An enthusiastic gathering almost filled the dingy hall and those present pledged themselves to support the proposed changes. The Borough Polytechnic led by its Chairman and Principal undertook to organise the new activities at an initial cost of £600 per annum to be met by the Technical Education Board. The Institute had been saved just in time."

I have an old photograph of the Institute which shows an enclosed wooden staircase outside the building. The L.C.C. ordered this to be built as an emergency fire escape to supplement the spiral staircase mentioned.

Mr. Arthur Anderson the founder of the Institute was one of the outstanding figures in the commercial life of the City a hundred years ago. He was born in Shetland in 1792, and started work as a beach boy at the age of ten. At 16 he was in the Navy, but left the service, walked from Portsmouth to London and became a clerk in the office of Mr. B. M. Willcox, a shipping agent. In seven years he was a partner. In 1837 he was instrumental in forming the Peninsular Steam Navigation Co., which developed into the P. & O. Line. He thereby controlled the largest and finest fleet of merchant ships in the world. He represented the Shetland Isles in Parliament 1847-53 and was a director of the Crystal Palace Co. He gave other institutes at Southampton and Lerwick. He and his wife resided for more than 40 years at "The Grove" now "Norwood Grove". He died 27th February, 1868.

The famous actress, Mrs. Patrick Campbell, made her first public appearance on a stage at the Institute with a concert party called "The Anomalies". Before this she had made an appearance on a private stage at the house of Mr. R. Fry in some amateur theatricals. At each appearance of "The Anomalies" the patronage grew and police were needed to regulate the private carriages which would line up the entire length on both sides of Chapel Road. This was in 1890. Three years later the name of this West Norwood lady was on the lips of every playgoer in London, for she had scored a great success as Paula in Pinero's *The Second Mrs. Tanqueray*. It was she who first uttered the word from the stage which made Eliza Doolittle and Bernard Shaw's *Pygmalion* an immediate success when performed in April, 1914, because of its "naughtiness". At one time (about 1893) she lived at No. 6, Uxbridge Villas, Paget Road, now known as No. 36, Tritton Road, and on the finger plate of the front parlour door she, being an amateur artist, painted a figure of Irving as Mephistopheles which was quite good and striking. Later she lived in Chatsworth Road. She died at Pau, in France, in April, 1940, at the age of 75.

Two little passage-ways near Maidstone Villas lead down to a little group of old cottages once called Orchard Cottages because of the fruit trees there. It is now Jaffray Place. Between these two passages stands a building once occupied by Mr. Mark Deacon, with his carpenter's shop on the upper floor. These premises were afterwards occupied by Mr. Naph Harris, a general dealer. Decorated with old firearms and wax figures in old-style Army uniforms, Mr. Harris's warehouse used to fascinate me as a small boy. On the other corner of Jaffray Place stands a little old-fashioned shop which, with the cottage next door, was part of original Norwood. The shop was occupied by Mr. Obee the builder. A similar pair of cottages stood where the four shops now stand. Mr. Abbot, a house-breaker, lived in one of the cottages by the corner of Victoria Place. Victoria Place, now called Weaver Walk, contains some old cottage property. Some of these cottages, known as Weaver's Cottages, built in 1845, were pulled down in 1938. This short turning is connected to Rothschild Street by a short passage-way which is closed every Good Friday to preserve the right-of-way which belong to the "Bricklayer's Arms". On Sunday mornings the "Bricklayer's Arms" was the meeting place of local cyclists with their penny-farthing bicycles. They used to hold a competition to see who could ride from the "Bricklayer's Arms" to the Gipsy House without getting off. Close to the "Bricklayer's Arms", opposite Ladas Road, you can still see the remains of the Norwood Brewery. This brewery was a flourishing business owned first by a Mr. Bennett, then by a family named Wadley, and finally by Mr. Cecil Beaton. The boiler-house was next to the road, and when the boilers needed replacing the authorities would not allow the new boilers to be installed so close to the pavement, and this I believe was the reason that the brewery had to close. Next to the brewery, a small row of houses, and then by the corner of Denmark Place was Mr. Deacon's ironmongery shop. Mr. Deacon was a builder as well, and his builder's workshop was at the side of his shop. It is now used as electrical works. In front of it stands a curious little structure on four iron wheels; it has stood there as long as anyone can remember, and has been used as a little shop and for other purposes. Denmark Place is another quiet little backwater of Norwood, built nearly a hundred years ago together with the row of small houses, Denmark Villas, facing the Congregational Chapel. Mr. William Openshaw, a son-in-law of Mr. Deacon, who was a Director of the Co-operative Wholesale Society, lived in one of these little houses all his married life.

Chapter 8
Elder Road

We will first survey the right-hand side of Elder Road, starting from the corner of Chapel Road, where was the baker's shop kept by Mr. W. W. Dove. Boys going to school would often stop to watch him icing wedding cakes in the side window. Mr. Dove had the contract for baking bread for the Convent. It was called plain bread, made in batches of about eight loaves to the batch, with no crust. The first two brick-built houses in Elder Road have typical old-fashioned windows on the ground floor. In the first house lived Mr. William Marsh, one of Norwood's two original policemen. Next come two little wooden-fronted shops also very old. One was occupied by Mr. Varney, a boot repairer, and the other by Mr. Ryman, greengrocer. The next shop, built out to the edge of the pavement was Mrs. Snelling's sweet shop, the tuck-shop of Elder Road school. Next door but one is the little one-storied "Ivy Cottage" occupied by Mr. Joseph Salmon, a nurseryman. I believe the house between Mrs. Snelling's shop and "Ivy Cottage" was built by Mr. Salmon for his son. Then come the three shops to the corner of Linton Grove one of which used to be occupied by a German boot-repairer, Mr. Schmidt, who invented a process for waterproofing leather. He displayed in his window a sheet of leather, hollowed in the middle and filled with water, to demonstrate his process. Mr. Hill, a general grocer, occupied the other shops.

Linton Grove was once a cul-de-sac, with thirteen houses on one side and the end blocked by a hedge behind which stood the Tivoli Nurseries. A hedge which enclosed the playing fields of the Lambeth Schools ran along the left-hand side of Linton Grove.

At the corner of Linton Grove and Elder Road stands the little St. Luke's School, which today looks even more like a village school than when it was first built in 1825. "Built on ground allotted to Archbishop Tenison's estate in Lambeth, a neat building for district schools for both sexes on Dr. Bell's educational system" says Allen's *History of Lambeth*. The left-hand portion of the building is part of the original school; the right-hand portion was rebuilt in 1908 and opened by Lord Halsbury. The original part of the school at the corner was two-storied, and on 13th April, 1901 part of the front wall fell into the street, on this was the inscription "Norwood National Schools 1825" and it was at this school that all Norwood children who were Church of England were educated. There was some rivalry between these children and the "Dissenting" children at the day school in Chapel Road. Periodically these National Schools were visited by government education inspectors who would examine the log book of the school, in which the head-mistress had to make a daily entry. By the kindness of Miss Norton, for many years head-mistress, and the Rev. Wilson Ruscoe, I was able to read the log book which has been faithfully kept every day since the school was opened. Many of the entries merely record—"Usual school routine", but others throw such a great light on life in the old days that they are worth repeating.

Dec. 16th 1862—Caution to the children concerning a quantity of mud near the school.

Feb. 26th 1863—Attendance small in the afternoon in consequence of the opening of a new building in the neighbourhood. (?)

March 10th 1863—Holiday on account of the marriage of the Prince of Wales.

March 24th 1863—30 of the elder children taken for a walk by the mistress from two till four o'clock.

May 7th 1863—Went to the house of Dr. Lester (Vicar of St. Luke's) in compliance with a note received to hear the decision of the Bishop concerning the management of the school.

June 22nd 1863—A paid monitor, E. Swaysland commenced her duties.

Aug. 18th 1863—Holiday in the afternoon. The Foresters walked in procession to the Crystal Palace.

March 1st 1864—The streets very muddy, consequently the younger children are unable to attend.

April 10th 1864—Attendance small in the afternoon owing to the following cause—General Garibaldi visited in the neighbourhood and the children were taken by their parents to see the General.
(While in England he stayed with Mr. A. Anderson at The Grove.)

July 15th 1864—School treat. 130 of the infants were taken to the field of S. W. Silver, Esq.

Aug. 18th 1864—Excursion to Hampton Court.

Aug. 31st 1864—Death of Miss Struddle the girls' school-mistress.

Sept. 6th 1864—School closed in respect of the above.

Nov. 10th 1864—Grace Alley, Chief Teacher, F. Hoare and S. Petty, pupil teachers.

Nov. 11th 1864—The usual holiday after inspection.

Dec. 23rd 1864—Christmas Holidays. Pupil teachers received their year's money.

March 20th 1866—This date being the day observed in Norwood as a time of humiliation and fasting for the cattle plague, 43 of the elder children taken to church.

1870—The Room begins to be inadequate for the needs of the neighbourhood.

1871—Since Christmas the number of children in attendance has been unusually small owing to the epidemic of small pox prevalent in the neighbourhood.

Feb. 27th 1871—Sent some notes to the Mothers asking for payment of school money owing.

(next day)—Cautioned the children against spending their school money.

Nov. 24th 1871—The fees of the school are raised one penny per child.

March 1st 1872—Holiday in honour of the Queen's visit to St. Paul's to return thanks for the restoration to health of H.R.H. Prince of Wales.

June 21st 1872—Haymaking commenced.

Dec. 1st 1876—Small pox prevalent in the neighbourhood.

Feb. 2nd 1877—Small pox very prevalent.

July 1894—Prince & Princess of Wales visited the Town.

April 13th 1901—School reopened this morning after the Easter holidays. School dismissed this afternoon owing to part of the front wall of the Upper Room falling into the street just after the children had assembled. No one injured. School visited in the afternoon by the District Surveyor and the Rev. Stansfield Prior.

April 16th 1901—Decided to close for remainder of week.

April 22nd 1901—School assembled but dismissed as Girls' rooms not in fit state to use.

May 2nd 1904—Notice received to say that the Schools are under the London County Council.

The fact that I do not mention any entries of school-boy, and schoolgirl misdeeds does not mean that there are no such entries. I omit them to avoid possible grandfatherly embarrassments.

Where the Lambeth Schools now stand was a large house called Elder Lodge. In the 1870's this was the residence of H.H. The Rajah Rampal Singh. The Rajah, so I have been told, was for some reason exiled from his native India by the Government, but I have no confirmation of this. His black servants were quite a picturesque feature of the neighbour-hood. The Ranee Rampal Singh died at Elder Lodge on the 1st March 1877, aged 28. The record of her funeral is in the books of my firm. The Rajah ordered her body to be embalmed and placed in a lead coffin with a glass lid. This coffin was put in the catacombs at Norwood Cemetery, and the Rajah often came to look at it. Elder Lodge stood approxi-mately where the Lambeth School Chapel now stands, almost next to the row of cottages named Maudslay Cottages, owned by Mr. Maudslay of Knight's Hill whose grounds reached down to the back of them. Mr. Peapell, well-known in Norwood as a postman, lived in one of these cottages. Next to Maudslay Cottages is the "Park Tavern", which was a plainly built old-world beer house with no out-standing features but much used because it was a bit out-of-the-way. It was rebuilt in the 1920s.

From the Park Tavern to the end of Elder Road is the present Elderwood House, the home for the aged poor. This building, delightful in its setting and restful to the eye, is one of the oldest buildings in Norwood. Built in 1815 it was the original Lambeth School for poor children, and was originally called "The Norwood House of Industry". Allen's *History of Lambeth* gives the following account of it:

"On the inclosure of waste ground at Norwood, some intelligent officers prevailed on the parish to purchase a piece of ground ... to build a house for the reception of poor children, (who were distributed about Norwood among the poor cottagers). Accordingly at a sale in 1809 they bought 1 acre, 3 roods, 13 perches for £277, and Mr. Roberts, boat-builder at Lambeth, gave a further piece of land making ... 2 acres in all which, being at the required distance from London they proceeded to build the house for pauper children. The whole expense including the purchase was about £4,000 and in 1812 there were about 200 children in the house. They are learned to read, knit, spin and weave cotton and mend their clothes and shoes. The present [1825] master and mistress, are Mr. and Mrs. Gibbs."

In 1945 I was asked by a film producing company if I could supply them with a photograph of the House of Industry for a film they were making on the History of Education. They told me that the Norwood House of Industry was the first Poor Law School in England, and that it was famous in those days as a training ground for pupil teachers. The present Lambeth School buildings were opened in 1885 at a cost of £56,000. There was sleeping accommodation for 650 children above the age of three. They were maintained until, at the age of 15, girls would enter domestic service, and at 14, boys could be apprenticed, or sent abroad into the Army and Navy. A separate building was the Infirmary, with an isolation ward. The children of school age attended the elementary schools in the neighbour-hood. A swimming pool was provided, and a feature of the school was the boys' brass band. What a picture they made as they marched down the High Street en route to the station for their annual seaside holiday! On Empire Day too, the boys' band would march to the various schools to play for the celebra-tions, while in the evening a large crowd would assemble in Norwood Park to watch displays by the boys and girls which included ceremonial marching, and folk and maypole dancing to the music of the band. The Lambeth School football team, too, was very hard to beat on its own pretty little ground behind the School Chapel. Mr. and Mrs. Stephen Morris were for many years Master and Matron of the Schools. There were also two popular Yard-masters, Mr. Nye, whose funeral in 1913 was preceded by the school band, and Mr. Cross, who was responsible for the school's fine record for sport and sportsmanship. The school evacuated at the beginning of the War in 1939, and has so far not returned to Norwood.

Now to review the other side of Elder Road starting from Gipsy Road corner. At the corner of Elder Road and Gipsy Road stood Clifton Lodge, the residence of the Russell family. Next to Clifton Lodge stood a little cottage where lived Mr. Harding the policeman. The first of the next three houses was occupied by the Bacon family for over a hundred years. Mr. Bacon's dairy was built at the rear and left side of the house. In the third house once lived Alice Rhodes, one of the four prisoners sentenced to death for the murder of Harriet Staunton at Penge. This trial was the first murder trial at Old Bailey, and was tried before Sir Henry Hawkins ("Hanging Hawkins") on the 19th September, 1877. Accused were Mr. and Mrs. Patrick Staunton, Mr. Louis Staunton, and Miss Alice Rhodes, two brothers and two sisters. Louis Staunton had married Harriet, the victim, in 1875. It was proved that she was not strong in the head, but she was heiress to £4,000. A child was born in March, 1876. Alice Rhodes looked after Harriet after the confine-ment. The Stauntons moved to Norwood in June, 1876. A love affair sprang up between Louis Staunton and Alice Rhodes. It was alleged that they sent Harriet and the child to the Patrick Staunton's at Cudham, Kent, and that there they were kept prisoner and starved. On April 8th, 1877 Patrick Staunton took the child to Guy's Hospital where it died the same night. On April 12th all four accused and Harriet arrived at Penge and booked lodgings. Next day a doctor was called and found Harriet beyond aid. She died and he gave a death certificate as "Primary cause of death—Cerebral disease, Secondary—Apoplexy". But a brother-in-law of Harriet overheard Louis asking in a shop whether he had to register the death at Penge or at Cudham. So he went to the doctor who then withdrew his certificate, and the police were called in. The trial lasted 7 days and the doctor's evidence filled 40 pages. All four were sentenced to death, a popular verdict. Then opinion changed. 700 doctors signed a petition that the post mortem and symptoms during life indicated brain disease and not starvation. Then the public doubted whether Alice Rhodes was in any way responsible. The case was re-opened by the Home Secretary (it was before the Court of Criminal Appeal). The Stauntons' sentence was changed to penal servitude, and Alice Rhodes was pardoned. One of the brothers died in prison, and Mrs. Patrick Staunton was released after a few years.

These three houses, together with Clifton Lodge were all demolished in 1947, and the new permanent prefabricated houses were built on the site of them. From this point, opposite Linton Grove, to the present Norwood Park, were fields known locally as the Twenty Acres, used by Mr. Bacon for grazing. In 1897 a site was granted by the Ecclesiastical Commissioners for the purpose of erecting a much-needed Parish Hall and Mission Room. The building, with seating for 200, was completed that year at a cost of £1,191. As a parish room it missed its mark, for the development of the southern end of the parish did not follow the lines that had been anticipated. On St. Paul's Day, 1926, the Vicar of St. Luke's dedicated the mission church in the name of St. Paul. A friend of mine, performing in an Army entertainment during the war of 1939–45 got into conversation with Datus, the famous "memory man" who was appearing in the same show. Learning that my friend came from West Norwood Datus recalled that on one occasion he was visiting this hall when some friends persuaded him to demonstrate his remarkable memory to the company there, the first time he had ever performed in public.

At the end of Elder Road, where Norwood Park is now, stood three little cottages. The first two were whitewashed with thatched roofs, and the one nearest Central Hill was a wooden cottage, called Boundary Cottage. With its out-buildings it stood in the middle of a strawberry garden, and was occupied by a family named Philbrook. The middle one of the three cottages was preserved by the L.C.C. as a storehouse when Norwood Park was laid out. By a mistake it was nearly pulled down, but the London Antiquarian Society took an interest in it and restored it at a cost of £200. It was once occupied by Mr. Veness, a turncock, and by a Mr. Lyon, a bookmaker. After surviving near-misses from bombs it suddenly caught fire on the 15th April, 1942, and was quickly burnt to the ground. The cottage which stood almost opposite to the "Park Tavern" was occupied by Mr. Cutting, and had several outbuildings attached to it. These cottages which stood well back from the road must have looked very picturesque in the old days with the River Effra flowing along the front of them. The occupants had to cross little wooden bridges over the stream to get to the roadway.

Norwood Park, or the "New Park" as it was first called, became a public park at the end of 1908. Sir Ernest and Lady Tritton made a large contribution towards the cost, and they also installed a fountain at their own expense. The park also contains a children's playground and a small pond. From the pond you get a fine view towards Dulwich and Sydenham, and you can see what remains of the trees of the once great North Wood.

I must mention the Relieving Office opposite Norwood Park in Elder Road. Mr. Street was Relieving Officer for many years. In early days, before this office was opened, people in receipt of outdoor relief had to walk to Lambeth Vestry at Kennington. Sometimes they fainted on the road with cold or lack of nourishment. In the wall on the Crown Dale side of this office is the flood mark I have already mentioned.

17

18

19

20

21

22

23

24

25

26

27

28

29

30

31

32

Chapter 9
Central Hill

Along the centre of Central Hill, once called Vicar's Oak Road, runs the boundary of the boroughs of Lambeth and Croydon, so by crossing this road one can walk out of London and into Surrey. At the bottom of Central Hill, opposite the end of Elder Road, a pair of iron gates opened upon a long carriage drive leading to a roomy mansion, with woodlands on either side, green lawns in front, and a poplar-girded pond through which flowed the Effra stream. An old print of the house bears the inscription—"View of Mrs. Mary Nesbitt's (late the Earl of Bristol's) Villa near the Horns in Norwood". On the Enclosure Act plan it is marked as belonging to "Mary Nesbitt". After Mrs. Nesbitt's occupation, it stood empty for a time, and was then purchased by a Mr. John Crawley, who turned it into the Park Hotel. The words—"John Crawley's Ales" could be seen through the paint on the walls of the house for many years afterwards. At that time the public were privileged to walk through the hotel grounds, pass through the wood, and emerge by a lane into Beulah Hill by Ivy Villa, later called "Ormsby". The Park Hotel was then purchased by Count Theodore D'Osseville, a nobleman of Normandy, whose daughter, Henriette, founded an orphanage there for Irish children after the great Irish famine of 1847.

How this came about can best be described from the following extracts from a series of articles entitled "The First Chaplain of Norwood Convent" published in the *Southwark Record*, the official monthly organ for the Roman Catholic diocese of Southwark, between August, 1929 and February, 1930. These articles were compiled from the convent records, which include letters written by the original nuns and from the unpublished journals of Father Vesque. In 1848 there was a threat of another revolution in France so . . .

"In the month of July 1848 Father Saulet set out secretly for England with the Superior of the Community of the Convent of the Orphans . . . the purpose of his journey was to assure a refuge for the religious in case of a new revolution. He had a letter of introduction to a Father Quiblier who was carrying on the duties of the Sacred Ministry in a suburb of London . . . at the epoch of which we are speaking the Dames of the Sacred Heart were the only religious who had a boarding school in the neighbourhood of London at Acton. There was not a single orphanage for girls, hardly any catholic schools, so the poor children had to enter the workhouse . . . where the priest had not the right of entry. . . . Mgr. Wiseman, welcomed with joy the project to found an establishment to receive poor little orphans and promised his protection. Preparations were made in the greatest secrecy. . . ."

At this time, a Mr. Manson had just built six houses on the right-hand side of Sydenham Grove, Lower Norwood (now Lansdowne Hill), and Mr. Manson let Father Quiblier have two of these houses, Mr. Manson himself residing in the one nearest to where the railway is now. Accordingly

"on the 13th September, 1848, Father Vesque, who was to be the first Chaplain of the Convent, Mother Ste. Marie (Henriette, the Foundress), and seventeen Nuns, embarked at Le Havre on the 'Colombine' for London and arrived there next day . . . the astonishment caused by the sight of eighteen Religious landing at the docks of London, in their white robes and black choir mantle, with their veils lowered is more easy to imagine than to describe . . . after a long wait the Religious were installed in two omnibuses and arrived at Sydenham Grove near Castle House where dwelt Father Quiblier . . ."

The article then goes on to give extracts from a letter written by one of the original sisters in which she describes the new dwelling, which was pulled down in 1949:

". . . possibly you would like the two patches of green grass in front of our doors, and the two graceful doorways held up by two columns on the top of some steps. Come along one of the two pathways which lead to these two entries. . . ."

The letter then goes on to describe how they and all their cases, etc., were piled into their small home, which was obviously too small for them all.

The article goes on:

"Three weeks went by thus and at last they learned that Park Hotel, a property situated not far away, had been bought after many difficulties. . . . From the time of George III, Park Hotel had been inhabited by the famous Mrs. Nesbitt, and the King used often to bring together his Ministers there for private business. Later on it became the rendezvous of the fashionable people of London during the season."

(It is interesting to note, in connection with this statement, that in the Penge Library is preserved an old Railway Guide in which is an advertisement for Mr. Crawley's Park Hotel which contains almost the same words.)

Then follows another letter describing the arrival at the Park Hotel . . .

"On Tuesday the 10th October it was decided that twelve of us would go to the Park Hotel and receive the cases whose contents would be arranged according to the different Offices. . . . The exterior of the house is simple and rather old-fashioned, but just look at those beautiful fields, it is as much as the eye can do to take in all the boundaries of the property. On one side is a wood, beyond are the trees which separate us from the road. There is a pool of water not far from the entrance with willows weeping on its edge . . . it is watered by a brooklet which flows along the foot of the hill. . . . Two fine salons, everywhere beautiful panelling, decorations on the ceiling, a lustre hanging in the middle and chimney pieces of marble which will soon disappear (this was to be the chapel) . . . our Sisters who had remained at Sydenham Grove did not rejoin us until after 5 o'clock, when they had cleaned up the house they took their meal, sitting on the ground, eating with their fingers, and having but one cup which they passed from one to another!!! (So ended the first day at the convent)."

The following instalments of these articles throw some very interesting light on the early history of the convent—

In 1849—

"a little stream which ran near the house overflowed its banks and flooded the kitchen to such an extent that the plates and food were floating about on the water and the fire was extinguished. Father Vesque had just returned from London when a Sister ran to tell him that the kitchen was full of water. He began by telling her calmly to put on some clogs, but as she insisted he went himself and saw that there was not a moment to lose . . . he did not know that in the passage there was a well ten feet deep and that planks which covered it had been washed away by the flood, he would have fallen into it had not Providence arranged that a portmanteau had floated out and covered up the opening."

In August 1849

"cholera raged in London and increased rapidly the number of orphans . . . later cholera passed over the doorstep of the Convent and five of the Religious fell victims to it (they all recovered). . . ."

In November 1850

"the promotion of Monsignor Wiseman to the cardinalate gave rise to anti-Catholic demonstrations by crowds in London. One of these crowds made its way towards the convent. Hearing the noise of drums the nuns looked out of the windows and saw the people carrying a guy dressed as the cardinal. The gate was closed, but some of the mob were already climbing over when the police arrived and succeeded in moving on the procession, which had to be satisfied with lighting a bonfire where it could be seen from the convent."

Again in 1850—

". . . a poor Irishman came to ask the nuns to take charge of his three children, all boys. It was explained to him that the nuns took girls only. He at once pointed out that this meant that his boys would have to go to a Protestant school and be brought up as Protestants. Realising the truth of this Father Vesque decided to open a school for boys in another part of the property . . ."

Thus began the little St. Joseph's Day School in Crown Dale, now no longer under the wing of the convent but administered by the Croydon education authorities.

Another important milestone in the history of the Norwood Convent is recorded thus:

"these Irish families, driven from their land by famine and disease, lived in mud huts. . . . Cholera was in the very life they led, and they died and were buried. But their children lived on. For them the workhouse, definitely Protestant, where Father Quiblier was refused admission, for the clergyman alone had the right to teach religion, and the Protestant Church must be attended compulsorily. And it was Norwood who came to the rescue to the utmost of its slender resources. . . . Mr. Doyle (a solicitor) who lived in the Convent lodge, realised the possibilities of the permissive law, due to Sir Stafford Northcote. He it was who made it known to the Catholic authorities. When it was pointed out that it was necessary that there should be accommodation for the children he was able to say that Norwood would build so as to provide for a hundred. . . ."

(The convent then added a new block to the main building.)

As a result of Sir Stafford Northcote's Bill (25 and 26 Vic. 43) all Nonconformists (which of course included Roman Catholics) were permitted to house their own poor law orphans providing they paid part of their upkeep. Catholic orphanages then sprang up, and Cardinal Wiseman said: "that never would the Catholic church in England forget what it owes to Norwood."

The following account of the convent and orphanage is taken from Walford's *Old and New London*, Vol. VI, p. 315.

"The Roman Catholic Orphanage of Our Lady, founded in 1848, is under the charge of a religious community of ladies. . . . The children, when placed in service, are watched over by the community, who give prizes annually to those who keep their situations longest, and can supply the best characters. . . . The institution is a branch from the Monastery de la Notre Dame des Orphelines, at La Delwrande in Normandy . . . The building here was commenced in 1855, and was erected from the design of Mr. Wardell. It is of Gothic design with a tower in the centre . . . a part of the edifice . . . is used as a boarding-school for young ladies of the higher classes."

The profits from this boarding school (which began with one pupil) were intended to help with the upkeep of the orphans. The school is called "Fidelis". The convent is no longer called the Monastery de la Notre Dame des Orphelines, its official name, but has become known as the Convent of the Faithful Virgin.

The woods at the back are marked on the Enclosure plan as the Great Pit Stake Coppice. Near these woods is the peaceful little burial ground. Among the many graves there is the grave of Bishop Michael Vesque (the first chaplain, who left Norwood to become Bishop of Dominica, where he died, his body being brought back to Norwood for burial). Next to his grave is the grave of his old friend Bishop Thomas Grant, first Roman Catholic Bishop of Southwark, who died in Rome and was by his own wish buried at Norwood next to his friend.

Opposite to the main convent buildings on Central Hill, in ground on which now stands the Borough Council's housing estate (known as the Bloomhall estate), stood Bloomfield Hall. It was once the residence of Mr. R. Hamilton. (Hamilton Road was named after him and Salters Hill was once Hamilton Hill.) In 1939 I had a letter from a Miss Hamilton, written from Canada, asking if Bloomfield Hall was still in existence. I sent her two photographs of it. In her reply she said—

"We are so pleased to have a picture of our great-grandfather's (Mr. Robert Hamilton's) house, Bloomfield Hall. It looks a delightful home. A cousin in America has sent to me an inventory of the pictures contained in the house about 1820. There were 480 of them, nearly all Old Masters."

Bloomfield Hall will always be associated with Sir Ernest Tritton, who was M.P. for Norwood. He was a partner in the firm of Brightwen & Co., and a director of the United Kingdom Provident Institution. He married Edith, second daughter of the late Frederick Green, Esq., in 1872. Each summer the Tritton family would entertain both the Norwood policemen and postmen with their families in the grounds of Bloomfield Hall.

Next to the grounds of Bloomfield Hall at the corner of Angel's Lane, now Roman Road, stood Ainsworth's school for young gentlemen, afterwards

Pope's. From there to the top of Gipsy Hill was just open common. By the side of the convent grounds runs Hermitage Road in which stands the Norwood Cottage Hospital, a very pleasing building opened in 1880. It was supported by voluntary contributions. At the back of the cottage hospital is a little colony of old houses known locally as "Newtown". It is a "walled city", for when it was built to accommodate the labourers who worked on the erection of the Crystal Palace it was surrounded by a wall to keep any unruly elements within bounds. In "Newtown" comprising Oxford Road, Naseby Road, Dover Road, and Eagle Hill, is a large mission hall which was erected at his own cost by Mr. J. Everett. In November, 1877 Mr. Everett on behalf of those worshipping there invited Mr. Walter Hobbs, a student at Spurgeon's College, to become Pastor. His ministry was much blessed, and membership reached 180, the congregation filling the hall. In 1880 Mr. Hobbs resigned, and afterwards became pastor of Gipsy Road Baptist Church. In more recent years other missionaries of "Newtown" have become Baptist ministers, the Rev. W. H. Teague becoming pastor of Central Hill Baptist Church, and the Rev. Percy Lake also became a minister. The mission is now under tbe pastoral oversight of St. Andrew's Presbyterian Church, Upper Norwood. Near the corner of Oxford Road and Central Hill was a house called Bernard Villa, and between there and Essex Grove stands a large building opened as a public house called the "Red Lion", the landlord being Mr. Bond. It was built by Mr. Masters who also built the Crystal Palace Hotel. It was then a girls' home before being converted into a block of flats. At the corner of Essex Grove stood Essex Lodge, said to have been a hunting lodge of the Earl of Essex. Whether this is true or not, we know that the Beulah Spa was opened in 1831 by the Countess of Essex (Kitty Clive, a famous actress) who died in 1834.

We have now entered the district of Upper Norwood and left West Norwood. My knowledge of Upper Norwood is not as extensive as my knowledge of West Norwood. However the two are so closely linked that it is impossible to separate them in a story like this. I shall not be able to give as many names of old residents and tradesmen who have played their part in the history of Upper Norwood, but at least I can include all the information available to me.

Continuing up Central Hill from Essex Lodge the next house of interest is charming little Effingham Lodge, No. 65 Central Hill, once occupied by Madame Tussaud of Waxworks fame. Between this part of Central Hill and Beulah Hill is the Upper Norwood Recreation Ground, opened by the Mayor of Croydon in 1890. About 12 acres in extent, it has a small pond and a bandstand. Between Harold Road and South Vale the houses included Central Hill Lodge, Rose Cottage, a young ladies' seminary, and Cedar Cottage. South Vale with a few old cottages was once no thoroughfare except for a footpath across the fields. At the corner of it stood Scotland House. Central Hill Baptist Church is the oldest Nonconformist church in Upper Norwood. It was erected in 1852 and enlarged in 1861. An old-fashioned caretaker's cottage, with half-circle windows, stood where Gatestone Road is now. A well-known pastor of the church was the Rev. S. A. Tipple. Between the church and the row of shops to the corner of Westow Street are some large old houses, one of which, called Mount Pleasant, did not look very pleasant with its high brick walls and large iron gates. The grounds of "Highlands" opposite were formerly the California Tea Gardens. The new police station at the corner of Highland Road was opened in April, 1940. I have read that the accommodation for delinquents is of the latest, with a push-bell to the office in case of need. It's a comforting thought.

Chapter 10
Westow Street and Church Road

From Central Hill we will turn right into Westow Street. It was described in 1852 as a very straggling street with cottages and shops all mixed up together, and still contains an odd assortment of shop and other premises. Like some of the roads of West Norwood it has many little backwaters, Melbourne Yard and Haynes Lane on the right side, and Paddock Gardens, Paddock Passage, Child's Lane, Carberry Road and Victory Place on the other. Taking the right-hand side first, at the corner of Central Hill used to stand an old-fashioned chemist's shop with two high bay windows, one in Central Hill and the other in Westow Street, kept at one time by a Mr. Ravis. It had a front garden, surrounded by a low wooden fence. Next door was a corn-chandler's shop occupied by Mr. Haynes. Then came a forge kept by Mr. Wheeler and one or two more little shops, and some fair-sized houses which were afterwards converted into shops. A large drapery establishment, Evans and Williams stood where the new Salvation Army Hall was built in 1926. The earlier Salvation Army Hall was at the end of Carberry Road. The Upper Norwood Salvation Army Corps was opened by Captain Polly Ashton and Lieutenant Jessie Butler in 1887. General William Booth, the Founder, visited the corps in 1888. The Upper Norwood Salvation Army Band is considered to be one of the finest in the organisation, and has broadcast many times. It was formed in 1889 with Herr von Schmidt as bandmaster. Later Mr. P. J. Baker was bandmaster for thirty-two years.

At the end of Westow Street a large residence called The Mount was once occupied by Sir George Sinclair and later by Lady Exeter. It is now the Royal Normal College for the Blind. Started through the exertions of Dr. Armitage and Dr. Campbell, who were both blind, on 1st March, 1872, the first school, which began with two pupils, was in three small houses in Paxton Terrace, Anerley Hill. The Mount was acquired in 1873, and the buildings were opened by Princess Louise in 1877. The Prince of Wales visited the College in the early 1920's. It is difficult to describe in words the wonderful work of teaching and training carried on at the Royal Normal College. One must pay a visit, as I have, to appreciate it properly. There you can see the very young pupils at their elementary lessons, the older ones giving grand displays in their gymnasiums, swimming in their lovely swimming bath, working in the carpenter's shop, and being trained to tune and repair pianos. When all this has been seen you can sit and listen to first-class music performed by the pupils in the concert hall.

The left-hand side of Westow Street begins with the public house the "Holly Bush", another wood-land name. The original "Holly Bush" stood a little back from the road, and had a very low front door. A feature of the old Westow Street was Mr. Carberry's little butcher's shop with small cottages adjoining. The Upper Norwood post office stands there now. Before West Norwood had its own post office Upper Norwood was the postal centre, and a staff of sixteen men had to cover the area from Herne Hill to Anerley. There were two deliveries a day, and the whole mail for the district could be put into a bag the size of those carried by present day postmen. A feature of the present Westow Street is the Foresters' Hall.

St. Andrew's Presbyterian Church was inaugurated in 1874. An iron church was erected and speedily filled. The foundation stone of the present building was laid 24th July, 1877. (What a year that must have been in Norwood; notice how many times it is mentioned in this story.) During the building of the church the congregation worshipped in the hall of the Blind College. The Rev. Robert Taylor was the first minister: he retired in 1892. The present minister, the Rev. Henry Martin, has been there for over 20 years now. The building is of brick, with handsome granite columns supporting the clerestory. It contains a beautiful organ built by Lewis under the supervision of Alfred Hollins, the famous blind organist.

At the corner of Westow Street and Church Road stands the "White Hart" hotel. An old picture of the "White Hart", described as the second best hotel, shows that it was a long wooden structure in 1858 with an old-fashioned bow window on the left side of the entrance porch, and a large bay window built out on the left-hand side of the upper storey. In front were chains and posts. The old swinging sign stood where the Upper Norwood war memorial now stands, and by the side of it was a pump which remained until about 1900. The water was sold at so much a pail. Belonging to the "White Hart" on the opposite (Church Road) side of the road were tea gardens entered under an archway made of the jaw-bones of a whale.

Church Road begins at the Royal Crystal Palace Hotel as it was called, built at the same time as the Crystal Palace. Just behind the hotel was the entrance to a large residence called Cintra. St. Aubyn's Church in Church Road is a fine building seating nearly a thousand, and St. Aubyn's Hall was the meeting place of many religious and philanthropic societies in the neighbourhood. It was badly damaged by a bomb in 1940. Between this church and the "White Hart" was the little Stoney Lane with several little old cottages now pulled down. They were over a hundred years old. The "Alma" public house was half in Croydon and half in

Penge. It is licensed by Penge.

In Belvedere Road is Grove Terrace, erected 1840–1 by the Porters Fellowship Benevolent Institute as almshouses for stevedores. There is a rumour that the late Prince Consort laid the foundation stone June, 1841 but there is no stone to substantiate this. It was apparently never used as almshouses but as private tenements. From here to All Saints' Church, Church Road has many large residences. Fox Hill and Sylvan Hill are names suggestive of the old woodlands. The Queen's Hotel has had many distinguished visitors including the Emperor Frederick of Germany. He came to England in 1887 to consult the famous doctor, Sir Morell Mackenzie about the illness that was to terminate his life. He was advised to stay on the Norwood hills as the pure air hereabouts would be beneficial. He stayed at the Queen's Hotel for six weeks.

Mr. John M. Cook, son of the originator of Cook's tours, lived at a pretty villa called Francesco, while at Rockmount, No. 88, lived a Mr. Eckford, a sweet pea specialist. The fields where Upper Beulah Hill is now were called the Church fields, and used as a short cut to Beulah Hill to avoid going round the church. An old wagon wheel was used as a stile there.

All Saints' Church stands on the highest ground in the district, 379 feet above sea level. The district was taken out of the ancient parish of Croydon in 1827. The church had seating accommodation for over a thousand. The Emperor Frederick of Germany worshipped there during his stay in Upper Norwood. The church was badly damaged by bombs during the last war. The church day schools are next to the church in Beulah Hill.

South Norwood Hill was once called Beggar's Hill. At the top was a public house called the "Windmill", much used for auction sales of land and property. On the hill stood a very large residence called Falkland Park, near the present Spurgeon's College. It was named after a former owner, Admiral Cary, Viscount Falkland. The original building stood between the college and the lodge. It had a tower which the admiral used to climb every morning to smoke a cigar and get the sea breezes. The grounds were extensive, and contained three ponds with rustic bridges. The present college building was the residence of Mr. Hay Walker, an American engineer.

Chapter 11
The Beulah Spa

The site of the old Beulah Spa was between Spa Hill, or Leather Bottle Lane as it used to be called, and Grange Road. The grounds, about 25 acres in extent, were at the back of Tivoli Lodge (no. 37 Beulah Hill) and the Lawns (no. 39). The site is now occupied by the All Nations Bible College. The surrounding districts abounded in mineral wells and springs. There were the wells at Sydenham, 12 in all, near the site of St. Saviour's Church, Taylors Lane, Wells Park Road. The Dulwich Wells at the corner of Lordship Lane and Dulwich Common. The Streatham Wells and a mineral spring in Biggin Hill. No-one knows exactly how Beulah Spa was first discovered. There is an old story, which may or may not be true, that a sick horse was turned out to graze in the field there and made such a miraculous recovery that the owner had the spring water analysed. The estate came into the hands of a Mr. John Davidson Smith, and it was he who first conceived the idea of laying out his portion of the Manor of Whitehorse for the purpose of rendering available the medicinal properties of the spring. He employed a famous architect, Decimus Burton, to convert the grounds into a place of recreation and entertainment, and work was begun about 1828. It was opened by the Countess of Essex in August, 1831. The waters were analysed by Professor Michael Faraday, the famous professor at the Royal Institution, one quart of the water yielding the following parts:

Sulphate of Magnesia	123
Sulphate of Soda & Magnesia	32
Muriate of Soda	19
Muriate of Magnesia	18½
Carbonate of Lime	15
Carbonate of Soda	3
	210½

Professor Faraday pronounced it: "One of the purest and strongest of the saline spas in the country, distinguished for the quantity of magnesia in it, resembling but far surpassing in this respect the Cheltenham waters." The water never freezes.

The grounds were entered by a rustic lodge which bore the legend—"No servants in livery or dogs permitted." The spa spring was housed in a thatched hut the shape of an Indian wigwam in the centre of which the water rose to a height of 15 feet, falling amidst a grotto of rocks. There were also a reading room, an orchestra, a camera obscura, a maze, a rosary, an archery ground, and a terrace from which lovely views were obtained. In arcades on either side of the octagonal reading room refreshments were served. A military band played each day during the season from 11 a.m. till dusk, and firework displays were also given there long before the days of fireworks at the Crystal Palace. Conveyance to town was by stage coaches to the Silver Cross at Charing Cross, running several times a day. The fares were 1/3d outside and 2/6d inside. The *Mirror* of April 1832 gives the following account of a visit to the Beulah Spa:

"We entered the grounds at an elegant rustic lodge, in the best taste of rusticity with the characteristic varieties of gable, dripstone, portico, bay window and embellished chimney. We descended by a winding path to a small glade at the highest part of which is a circular rustic building used as a confectionery and reading room near which is the Spa within a thatched apartment. Water is drawn by a contrivance at once ingenious and novel. A glass urn-shaped pail, terminating with a cock of the same material and having a stout rim and cross-handle of silver, is attached to a thick worsted rope and let down into the spring by a pulley, when the vessel being taken up full, the water is drawn off by the cock."

Three separate guides to the spa were published between 1832 and 1838; they are preserved in the British Museum. From the guide books we learn that the price of admission was one shilling on ordinary days and 2/6d on fete days. The yearly subscription for a family was three guineas, and for one person a guinea and a half. Among the fetes held there was one for the Freemasons' Girls School in 1839 under the patronage of the Queen Dowager. Readers of Thackeray will not have forgotten the charity fete devised by Lady de Sudley on behalf of the British Washerwomen's Orphan Homes which figures in Cox's diary. In 1834 the Duke of Gloucester visited the spa to drink the waters. Thus the spa was simply a place of popular amusement, and we may suspect that any cures effected were more by the healthy open air than by the mineral waters. Its popularity soon waned. On the 5th June 1835 the Whitehorse estate, including the spa, was put up to auction. The purchaser, Mr. Atkinson, renovated the grounds, which were still open in 1854, but were described as being all now more or less decayed and neglected.

Chapter 12
Beulah Hill

Mr. Alfred S. Foord, speaking of the Beulah Spa in his book, *Springs, Streams and Spas of London* says that on the Enclosure Act plan Beulah Hill appears as Beaulieu Hill. This is not correct. The Upper Norwood Enclosure plan shows the road, but it is not named at all. On the Lower Norwood Enclosure plan Beaulieu Hill is marked at the top of Central Hill and Gipsy Hill. Allen, in his *History of Lambeth*, mentions Beaulieu Hill as being the present Crystal Palace Parade. The English Place-name Society's volume on Surrey, page 49, regarding the derivation of "Beulah", gives the form "Beule-stret" in 1359 (Calendar of Close Rolls), with "beau lieu", beautiful spot, as a possible origin. John Gorton's *Topographical Dictionary*, 1833, vol. III, page 75, under "Norwood, co. Surrey", refers to Norwood Beaulieu Hill, so called to distinguish it from Lower Norwood, and to:

> "the discovery of a mineral spring which issues from the brow of a hill at Beulah, or Beaulieu, the estate of J. D. Smith, Esq."

On the Enclosure plan, the actual site of the Beulah Spa is marked as Bewlys Coppice. We may read that:

> "a large plot of ground adjoining the grounds of the Spa has been laid out for the building of the new town of Beulah, the increasing popularity of the place demanding the erection of suitable residences for such as wish to render this beautiful spot a place of permanent abode".

There can be no doubt that Beulah Hill is a beautiful residential road, now alas, rapidly changing its character as modern villas and blocks of flats spring up everywhere. I do so hope that future development will preserve the fine trees which add so much to the beauty of the surroundings.

Beulah Hill is full of interest and in walking along it we shall pass many fine houses which have been occupied by notable residents. At the corner of Grange Road opposite All Saints' day school, is Grange Mount, once the residence of the famous tenor vocalist, Mr. Sims Reeves. A later occupant was Sir William P. Treloar, J.P., Lord Mayor of London for 1907, well known as the benefactor of crippled children. The great musician Mendelssohn twice visited Beulah Hill. He was the guest of Thomas Attwood, organist of St. Paul's Cathedral, at his house Roselawn in 1829 and again in 1832. Here it was he composed his Evening Bell with part of his "Son and Stranger" and the E minor "Capriccio", the MSS. of which are all dated "Norwood, Surrey, November 1829".

In Spa Hill there were some very old cottages and a small beer house, the "Leather Bottle". At the corner of Spa Hill and Beulah Hill stood the "Beulah Spa Tavern", a small public house with stabling at the side. Next to it was the fine "Beulah Spa Hotel", built to accommodate visitors to the spa. It was pulled down in 1937 together with the adjoining "Beulah Spa

Tavern", which has now been rebuilt on very modern lines. Opposite the "Beulah Spa Hotel", at No. 32 Beulah Hill, lived Mr. T. W. Stoughton, son of Dr. Stoughton, and a partner in the well-known publishing firm of Hodder and Stoughton.

A few yards from the Beulah Spa Hotel was the gateway of a drive leading to No. 49, a fine mansion named Westwood, the residence of the famous Baptist preacher, the Rev. Charles Haddon Spurgeon. This fine mansion stood well back from the road in grounds of about 10 acres. On one side of the house was a square tower, and on the other side was a round tower surmounted by a balustrade. The interior of the house was also impressive. The drawing room was forty feet in length, there was an extensive conservatory and fernery, and the charming boudoir, with its painted ceiling, walls and cornices, was the handiwork of Mrs. Spurgeon. In the grounds was the "Question Oak" under which Mr. Spurgeon used to hold levees of his students for the purpose of answering all the most difficult questions they could ply him with. Also the summer-house in which he wrote many of his works. After the death of Mrs. Spurgeon the house was purchased by a Mr. Arthur Ross in 1905. The mansion was pulled down about same the time as the "Beulah Spa Hotel". A new road which follows the line of the old front drive to Westwood is called Spurgeon Road, thus commemorating the association.

A few yards from there on the bend in the road stands a rather rambling large red-brick house built right out to the edge of the pavement, called Little Menlow. Here lived Colonel Gourard, representative in England of the famous inventor Edison. Mrs. Stoughton told me once that this was the first house in England to have a telephone. Wires were carried on poles from this house to the Crystal Palace, and visitors to the exhibition were able to speak from there to Colonel Gourard in his house.

Almost opposite to Little Menlow is a house called St. Valery, once the residence of Mr. Bob Lee, a well-known bookmaker. The house that I personally like best on Beulah Hill is a lovely old Georgian house called The Yews which stands at the corner of a little lane nearly opposite to where Hermitage Road joins Beulah Hill. Its bowed frontage and windows are a delight. The lane at the side of it led to Mr. Pringle's nursery. Another fine old house in this part of Beulah Hill is The Priory, a large old house lying well back from the road almost hidden by trees.

Where Convent Hill now joins Beulah Hill stood a little four-roomed, one-storied dwelling called Rose Cottage, with a creamery attached. Here some sixty years ago people would come in large numbers in the summer to partake of the strawberries that grew in the strawberry gardens. You could eat as many as you liked for 6d, children 3d. Mr. Thompson who farmed the gardens kept his own cows to supply the cream for the fruit. In more recent years it was farmed by Mr. George Mustoe, and I have pleasant recollections of playing football in the field at the back of it, abutting on to the Convent woods. It is all built over now.

Next door to Rose Cottage stood a large old house known as the Deerfield. Tradition says that this was a hunting box used by William IV. This may or may not be true, but a certain amount of hunting undoubtedly did take place in the neighbourhood. But I do know that it was a very curious house, for I once went over it. There was a curious little "secret" staircase in a small cupboard by a fireplace in an upper room, which led down to one of the rooms on the ground floor. Under the house there were more cellars than there were rooms in the house, while from these cellars there was a short tunnel leading towards Beulah Hill under the front lawn: it came to a dead end. The occupants of the house told me that a lost kitten led them to discover that the stable had a double wall with quite a space between it. It seemed to me to be a house which ought to have a history, and all sorts of tales could have been invented about it. I can remember that an old goat tethered to a long chain on the front lawn scared the life out of me as I left the house in the darkness of a winter's night.

On the other side of the road, close to the corner of Biggin Hill, stood a house called Springfield which was demolished in 1906. It was once occupied by Mr. Townsend who was fond of entertaining the literary giants of his day. Charles Dickens was always a welcome visitor, and it was at Springfield that he set the scene of the meeting between David Copperfield and Dora Spenlow. It is generally agreed that David Copperfield is an autobiography of the author's own life, and Charles Dickens must have been well acquainted with Norwood as the following extracts from David Copperfield prove:

Chap. 26—"My very carpet bag was an object of veneration to the Clerks to whom the house at Norwood was a sacred mystery."

Chap. 33—"The first thing I did on my own account, when I came back, was to take a night walk to Norwood to go round and round the house, without touching the house, thinking of Dora."

"I was soon as well known on the Norwood Road as the postman on that beat."

"I provided and sent down by the Norwood Coach the night before a delicate little hamper."

"At six in the morning I was in Covent Garden buying a bouquet for Dora. At ten I was on horseback with the bouquet in my hat to keep it fresh, trotting down to Norwood."

Turning down Biggin Hill, the first house on the left is White Lodge, once the residence of Sir August Manns, the conductor of the Crystal Palace orchestra. In the grounds of White Lodge is the mineral spring I have mentioned before, after which the house Springfield was named. On the Enclosure map of 1800 this spring is marked, whereas the Beulah Spa spring is not. The water gushed up at a rate of several gallons a minute. It undoubtedly taps the same spring that used to come out at the bottom of Biggin Hill beyond the small tenement houses, where the water used to run out of a culvert into a pond. It was blocked by the sanitary authorities in 1898, but there is still some of the masonry in existence.

A little further down Biggin Hill from White Lodge on the opposite side, a small roadway led to Bigginwood House, the residence of Mr. James Epps, whose cocoa, "Grateful & Comforting", was well known. The last time I saw it in 1938 the old house stood an empty ruin, its walls blackened by a recent fire. As I walked through the thick undergrowth of the woods which surrounded it I thought what a lovely spot it must have been in its heyday. The modern red brick house at the corner of Biggin Hill and Beulah Hill was built by Mr. Epps for his son.

A feature of Beulah Hill is the pond, now a rather ornamental pond but once just a watering place for horses and cattle, with a railing across the middle to prevent the animals getting into deeper water. It was called locally the Big Pond, and when frozen was used for skating. Then there was a scene of much fun and merriment, men with chairs offering to put skates on for a few coppers, and baked potato and roast chestnut barrows with their cheerful fires stood around. In those days of hard winters it was usual to get a few weeks' skating, and the ironmongers always had a good stock of skates.

The "Conquering Hero" had been rendered over with cement which has taken away some of its old character. I used to wonder if the name "Conquering Hero" had anything to do with the victorious General Garibaldi's visit to the Grove in 1864. But an old resident of Beulah Hill told me that it got its name in a different way. Beulah Hill was a high-class residential road, and the residents were horrified when it was proposed to build a public house there, and did everything in their power to prevent it. The brewer, however, had his way, the public house was built, and the sign, the "Conquering Hero", was raised in defiance. By the side of the public house was a shop occupied by Mr. Carnham, a builder.

Almost opposite is Gibsons Hill with Arnulls Road turning off it, both marked on the Enclosure Map of 1800. Both roads contain some fine old houses, while at the far end of Arnulls Road are a few quaint cottages, some having outside staircases leading to the upper rooms. Leafield, the first house on the left in Gibsons Hill, was occupied by the Misses Leaf. These ladies were greatly interested in temperance work, and had a hall built in their grounds for the use of local Bands of Hope, etc. Half-way down Gibson's Hill was a gate crossing the lane leading to Green Lanes, Norbury, an ancient land near which Roman coins have been dug up. By the gate a bridle path led to The Grove, occupied by Mr. A. Anderson, and later by Fredk. Nettlefold, Esq. Opposite The Grove stood The Hollies standing in a large meadow which extended from Gibson's Hill to Streatham Common. At the side of the meadow in Gibson's Hill was a small gateway leading to two large houses with lawns in front. On the right-hand side at the bottom of the lane leading to Green Lanes stood Biggin Hill Farm.

Near the corner of Gibson's Hill was Grecian Villa, the residence of R. H. Fry, Esq. Dick Fry was a famous bookmaker, and it is said that millions of pounds passed through his hands. He was a liberal supporter of all local charities and societies. He died at Grecian Villa on the 22nd December 1902, aged 66 years, and was buried at Norwood Cemetery. Grecian Villa is now part of St. Joseph's College, and has been altered beyond recognition. A red brick church has been built at the side, and it in no way conforms with the character of the old residence. The fine grounds are converted into sports fields for the scholars. Leafield has also been bought by the college authorites. Grecian Crescent was named after Mr. Fry's house. From the corner of the Crescent to the corner of Crown Hill stood some large old detached houses similar to those still standing round the corner in Crown Hill. Mr. Covington used to live on the corner. These old houses were demolished in 1938 to make way for the modern block of flats and shops known as Crown Point. Bonnicot, a pretty little house standing at the corner of Grecian Crescent, was demolished by a bomb in 1940.

Before I leave Beulah Hill, I must mention The Lads' Rest, No. 106, Beulah Hill. The Lads' Rest was originally a holiday home for the poor street arabs of Whitechapel, but in 1888 the necessity arose for retaining some orphan boys in the home until they were of an age to earn their own living. The boys were received between the ages of 8 and 10 leaving when they were 15.

I must also mention the carriers, Mr. Howard and Mr. Keene, who before the days of the London Parcel Delivery Co. later Carter Paterson & Co., used to start from Beulah Hill, calling at the private houses and shops to collect orders for Town. They started about mid-day and did not return until midnight. The required goods were delivered on the up journey following morning.

"Billy Foyle's Fire Brigade" also deserves mention. The funny old fire engine used to stand at the corner of Crown Lane. Billy Foyle raised subscriptions for this among the residents in the vicinity, and it was a volunteer brigade, but I don't think it was ever called upon to volunteer for anything in the way of fires, which perhaps was just as well.

Chapter 13
Crown Dale and Crown Lane

Starting from the bottom of Crown Dale, or Crown Hill as it used to be more correctly called, is a row of old houses facing the little St. Joseph's day school, next door to which is a small house once occupied by Mr. Doyle and later the presbytery of the convent. From this house an old hedge bordering on allotments ran to the corner of Queen's Road, now Queen Mary Road. In June 1935 the Croydon Council purchased this 6½ acres of allotment ground for about £6,000. The old hedge then disappeared and new roads and modern houses sprang up. From Queen's Road to the corner of Beulah Hill stood the large houses already referred to. Two residents of these houses were Mrs. Franks and Josiah Temple, Esq. (whose house is still called Temple's Orchard), both well known and actively engaged in promoting the welfare of Norwood. Opposite Queen's Road was the builder's premises of Mr. Fox, below which was Mr. Alexander Smith's nursery and a row of small cottages which were probably among the oldest in Norwood. They and the nursery were all demolished by a flying-bomb in June 1944, and the whole of this area to the corner of Knight's Hill as far as Furneaux Avenue is being cleared to make way for a new Borough Council housing estate. From Mr. Smith's nursery to the top of Crown Dale were several large old houses. Next to the nursery was Beauchamp Cottage, standing well back from the road. Two others were Clifford Lodge and Clifford House, the latter once the residence of the parents of Sir John Hunter, Surgeon-General to the British Force in the Egyptian campaign. At May Cot lived Madame Helena Petrovna Blavatsky. Of Russian birth, she was the founder of the Theosophical Society, the influence of which changed the religious and scientific thought of the age, says one authority, though she was stigmatised by another learned society as a charlatan. She was the author of *The Secret Doctrine*, *The Key to Theosophy*, etc. She died in 1891 aged 60 years.

Over the cross-roads and into Crown Lane. At the corner of Crown Lane and Beulah Hill stood the shop, warehouse, and stables of Mr. Preddy, a corn-chandler. The row of shops which stood facing the "Rose and Crown" were called Crown Place, some of them were demolished by the bomb which destroyed the "Rose and Crown" in October 1940. In the middle of these shops was the old forge. A small beer-house with the village pound at the side stood on the site of the "Rose and Crown." In front of the "Rose and Crown" was a horse trough, and at the back of it was Nightingall's riding stables. The little shops next to the public house were all destroyed by the bomb, which made a direct hit on the "Rose and Crown", causing the heaviest casualties of all the bombing incidents in West Norwood.

Where the Home for Incurables now stands was a large rambling one-storied house, Norwood Lodge, the residence of Mr. Joseph Maudslay, partner in the famous engineering firm of Maudslay Bros., marine engineers. Later it became the residence of Mr. S. W. Silver, the founder of Silvertown. The British Home for Incurables was one of the earliest institutions of its kind in England. It was founded in 1861 by a few generous men. They were at that time only able to give pensions of £18 per annum, and medical attention to five out-patients. In less than six months the number was doubled, and premises were taken in Clapham Road which until 1894 formed the local habitation of the charity. Funds steadily increased and the institution was fortunate in securing the sympathy of H.R.H. the Princess of Wales who became a patroness shortly after her marriage in 1863, the first charity in Great Britain to receive her patronage. The lease of the old premises ran out, and the committee were unable to buy the freehold. So the site in Crown Lane was secured, and the fine new buildings were erected at a cost of £27,500, excluding the chapel. The building was opened 3rd July 1894 by H.R.H. the Princess of Wales. A small but pretty chapel was built, the gift of the late Miss Leicester, and in 1899 a new wing with a fine entertainment hall was erected. In 1939 another new wing was added for the accommodation of patients and staff. There is another Home for Incurables at Putney. Opposite the Home is the Norwood Reservoir of the Metropolitan Water Board, which supplies the district with water. The rest of Crown Lane consisted of fine large residences, many of which are now disappearing to make way for smaller houses and blocks of flats. After the Home for Incurables came Pierremont, St. Mary's (used as a children's home before the war of 1939–45), Burlington Lodge, and Crown Lane End (now Crown Lane Gardens).

Here Crown Lane becomes Streatham Common North Side. The first house, Winton Lodge, a long low, pretty little house with trellis on the walls for climbing roses, was the residence of Col. Sir Herbt. J. F. Parsons, Bart., who I believe was connected with "Phospherine". Then Esam Lodge, South Hill, the residence of the late Bruce Penny, Esq. Town, Clerk of Lambeth; Warrington Lodge; Gresham Lodge; White Lodge, the residence of the Rev. Thomas Greenwood, a well-known Baptist minister; Oak Lodge; and Fern Lodge at the corner of Leigham Court Road. On the opposite corner was Bens Hurst, the residence of Canon Carver, Master of Dulwich College, and next door was the fine residence of the Tate family, well-known in connection with sugar. The house was called Park Hill. It was also once the residence of the Leaf family, silk mercers in Old Change. In more recent times it has been St. Michael's Convent. On the corner of Streatham Common stood a large house called Jerviston Lodge, with grounds extending down the side of Ryecroft Road.

"Take the children to Streatham Common; they will get the air straight from Brighton up there." This was old Dr. Samuel Welch's advice to my mother. Certainly Streatham Common is a healthy spot, and it is a favourite with Norwood folk. In Domesday Book, Streatham is spelt Estreham, and has been variously spelt Stretham, Streetham or Streteham. Curiously enough this common, 66 acres in extent, was in the Manor of Vauxhall, or Fauxhall as it was once called. Vauxhall of course is some miles away, but this is by no means an isolated case of the dismemberment of manors. I have already mentioned the district of Penge as belonging to the Manor of Battersea. The upper portion of the common was formerly called Lime Common, and is covered with dense undergrowth. Brambles, furze and bracken flourish here. The lower part of the common is open and available for games. The cricket ground is guarded by posts and chains, and is specially reserved for local clubs under the Metropolitan Commons Act 1884. There are two ponds, a small bandstand, and a horse ride. A very old view of the common shows a small cottage close to the pond. There was formerly a cage on the common erected between 1740 and 1760 for the confinement of loose and disorderly persons. The common has been the scene of some petty riots arising from the encroachment of the lord of the manor on the rights of the tenants. On one occasion a mob met on the common and set the furze on fire. It seems that the Duke of Bedford used to let the poor have the furze, but that year, 1794, he sold it for £80. (Arnold's *History of Streatham*.)

By the side of the common is The Rookery with its lovely gardens taken over by the L.C.C. The Rookery, a large house once the residence of Sir Kingsmill Key, is noted for the celebrated Streatham Wells. The first account of these mineral springs is given by Aubrey. Writing in 1673 he says:

"The medicinal springs here are in the ground east of the common, they have a mawkish taste. They were first discovered about 14 years back and this is the third year they have been commonly drank."
(History of Surrey).

Streatham Spa soon became fashionable, the natural beauties of Streatham Common adding to the attraction. The reputation of the wells was at its height at the beginning of the 18th century. In the height of the season concerts were given twice a week. The use of the waters was by no means confined to the locality as will be seen from the following advertisement:

"The true Streatham waters, fresh every morning, only at Child's Coffee House in St. Paul's Churchyard, Nando's Coffee House near Temple Bar, the Garter Coffee House behind the Royal Exchange, the Salmon and at the Two Black Boys in Stocks market. Whoever buys it at any other place will be imposed upon.

(Postboy 8 June 1717)."

Assemblies are mentioned as being held in connection with the wells as late as 1755. After about 1792 the spring was closed. This final closing of the old spring caused people to turn their attention to another spring of a similar kind which had been discovered at the end of the 18th century about half a mile away.

Mr. Alfred S. Foord in his book says:

"Most writers from Lysons onwards fail to make it sufficiently clear that the medicinal well in the Valley Road is quite distinct from, and was in fact discovered more than a century and a half after the original springs at the Rookery."

These wells in Valley Road were at the back of what is now the United Dairies premises opposite Wellfield Road, named after them. The tea gardens attached to the Valley Road wells were used down to the 1860's. The house itself is a plain building of brick faced with stucco, and having a bust of Aesculapius over the doorway. On the north side of the house, and forming an annexe to it, is a room containing the pump over the well. The water rises at a temperature of 52° Fahrenheit. When pumped up it has a slight smell of sulphur, and is sparkling and bright, and not unpleasant to the taste. Although it contains an appreciable amount of iron, causing an ochreous deposit on the pumping apparatus, it cannot properly be classed as chalybeate. There is in the Guildhall Library an Indian ink drawing of the house. The Curtis family have according to the rate books occupied these premises since the year 1875.

At the back of these wells in Valley Road were the fields known locally as The Five Fields, now built over, stretching up to Leigham Court Road, named after the Manor of Leigham Court. "This manor," (as it was then called says) Brayley's *History of Surrey* (1850), Vol. 3, p. 430, "appears to have been granted by Ela, wife of Jordan de Sackville, to the prior and convent of Bermondsey in 1152." After many changes it was transferred to John Howland, Esq. of Streatham in 1610, and eventually passed into the possession of the Duke of St. Albans who sold it to Lord Thurlow in 1789. It was by this time known as the Manor of Leigham Court, and was purchased from the devisees of Lord Thurlow by Beriah Drew, Esq. of Streatham in 1836, together with 233 acres of land. In 1839 that gentleman was at the expense of making Leigham Court Road through the estate from Streatham High Road to a point where St. Julian's Farm Road is now. The continuation of the road up to Streatham Common was from its inception up to about 50 years ago under the name of St. Julian's Road. In order to avoid confusion with St. Julian's Farm Road the name of Leigham Court Road was given to its entirety. In Leigham Court Road, a high class residential road now rapidly changing its character, is St. Peter's Church, built about 1870. The Rev. H. Baron Dickinson, M.A., the Rev. M. Jarvis, and the Rev. Father Morson were all very popular vicars of this church.

Chapter 14
Knight's Hill

Having strayed a little in this story we must now return to Crown Lane, and we will continue our walk from here down Knight's Hill, formerly Knight's Hill Road. Knight's Hill takes its name from the family of Thomas Knyght, mentioned in a document of 1545. (*Place-names of Surrey*, p. 34.)

Starting from the top, the building at the corner of Crown Dale was the original Norwood post office. When the inhabitants of Norwood petitioned for a post office it was placed at this extremity of the district. Was this because the postal authorities thought that only the wealthier residents of Beulah Hill would be capable of writing letters? The first postmaster was Mr. John Gardiner, who is reported as not possessing the politeness necessary for a shop-keeper. Stamps were sold through a small window like a railway booking office window to people standing outside. Next to the post office was a small piece of ground on which a tiny shop was erected by a Mr. Jack Blunden who used to sell winkles there. The next shops were called Clifford Place; the name Clifford also appears in the names of two houses round the corner in Crown Dale.

On the other side of the road at the corner of Crown Lane stood a little shop kept by Mr. Rose, the builder. Mr. Rose, I have read, brought his bride there on horseback, sitting pillion in front of her husband. The next shop was a grocer's, Mr. Pretty, and then comes another little backwater with some small cottages called Dibdin's Cottages, named after the well-known family of Dibdin. Miss Emily Dibdin, who died at 307 Beulah Hill in 1938, aged 83, was great-grand-daughter of Charles Dibdin, 18th century actor, musician, poet and playwright who, amongst over nine hundred songs, wrote the still famous "Tom Bowling". Her father was the Rev. Robert Wm. Dibdin, and of her brothers, Sir Robert, the eldest, was a President of the Law Society, Charles was founder of the Civil Service Lifeboat Institute, and died two weeks before he was to receive a knighthood. Sir Lewis Dibdin was Dean of Arches and Vicar-General of Canterbury, and Edward R. Dibdin was Curator of the Walker Art Gallery at Liverpool.

From Dibdin's Cottages a few more shops bring us to Norwood Cottage which was a nice old house, the residence of Mr. Willcox, the builder, whose mother kept a little toy shop next door. After Mr. Willcox died the house was converted into a petrol station, and the alterations completely spoiled the charm of the old house. Next door is The Bays, a similar house somewhat hidden by shrubs and trees. It has been the abode of a succession of doctors, beginning with Dr. Sharp (who shared the medical practice of Norwood with Dr. Chapman of Norwood Road), and ending with Dr. Smallwood. By the side

of this house was a piece of waste ground on which the Borough Council have laid out a small housing estate. Then come two or three old houses, the first of which was incorporated in Carl Hentschel's photo-engraving works. These works afterwards moved to Wolfington Road. Carl Hentschel, the "father" of process engraving, was the original of "Harris" in Jerome K. Jerome's famous story, *Three Men in a Boat*. In the house next door but one to Carl Hentschel's works stained glass windows were made. Next door to this house, in large grounds, was a big house called Portobello, with a semi-circular drive in front of it. At the lower end of this drive was a small lodge, while at the upper end was an ugly building with a story attached to it. Mr. Quilter, who lived at Portobello, had a bitter quarrel with his neighbour opposite, Mr. Thomas Maudslay, a brother of Mr. Joseph Maudslay of Crown Lane, and a partner in the same engineering works. As a result of this quarrel, Mr. Quilter erected this building, which was an exact replica of the entrance to Maudslay's engineering works, right facing Mr. Maudslay's private residence so that every morning, including Sundays, when he looked from his front windows, Mr. Maudslay saw his works staring him in the face. Local legend? No, you can still see the row of evergreen trees which Mr. Maudslay planted in the front of his house to hide this ugly building from his view. Those who can remember Mr. Maudslay's house will recall the conservatory which he built on its roof where he could sit and overlook it. Many local men worked at Maudslay's works, and my grandfather remembered the engineering works of Maudslay Bros. in Westminster Bridge Road. Mr. Maudslay's house was then called Knight's Hill House, but later it was called Holderness House, and it stood where the Knight's Hill playing field is now. Its grounds stretched down to Elder Road and southward to Crown Hill. I have been told that the two men afterwards made up the quarrel, and that Mr. Quilter offered to remove the offending building, but Mr. Maudslay would not hear of it. Portobello House has now been pulled down together with this gateway, and in this year 1949 the Borough Council is building an extensive housing estate on the site of it. Next to Portobello were two semi-detached residences, Ivy Villas, still there, and the house which was converted into the Lambeth Maternity Home, with 4 wards and 22 beds. Some 450 babies were born in this house every year until it was evacuated during the war of 1939–45.

From this spot, all the way down to the present Wolfington Road, this side of Knight's Hill was covered with the fields of the St. John's Lodge estate, which covered all the area between Knight's Hill and

Leigham Court Road. The roads which now cover this area are still referred to by the older inhabitants as "The Estate". St. John's Lodge estate, once occupied by an Indian family named Colvin, became known as Treadwell's Farm because this farm estate was purchased by a Mr. Treadwell who, I believe made a fortune contracting for the construction of railways. No-one seems to remember the exact spot on which the farm-house stood, but as far as I can ascertain, it was near the corner of Thurlestone Road and St. Julian's Farm Road. Where Casewick Road now runs between Thornlaw Road and Wolfington Road was a small row of farm labourers' cottages, attached to the farm, called Thornback Row. Opposite these cottages was the stackyard of the farm. There was a pond on the farm by the present tennis courts at the bottom of Cheviot Road, and the paddock was where the present Brotherhood buildings now stand. The path that encircled the farm was known as the Mile Walk. Water for the farm was drawn from a well reputed to be 100 feet deep by a horse harnessed to a long arm or bar which he pulled round and round like a capstan. On the farm estate Mr. Treadwell built a miniature railway with a small steam locomotive behind which many local boys were treated to a ride. It ran round a circular track. A plot of land on the farm estate, near the present Bewlys Road is marked on Mr. Driver's map of Lambeth Manor 1806 with the word "Julians", hence the name St. Julian's Farm Road.

Now to return to Mr. Maudslay's house, on the other side of Knight's Hill. Next door to it, down the hill, stood a large house called Burton Dassett, once occupied by Mr. Jules Levy, a famous cornet soloist. Dassett Road is named after it. At the corner of Darlington Road, once called Durham Road, stands a house of no great age, Silverdale. There is a local story that this house was once put up for auction, and a local builder offered only £65 as a first bid. It was knocked down to him at this price because everyone present was too overcome with laughter to offer a higher bid. Just behind this house in Darlington Road stood a large house built entirely of concrete with a castle-like tower. It was called Meadow Bank, and was the residence of a Captain Fawcett who served under Nelson. An artist friend of Captain Fawcett painted naval battle scenes on the ceilings. This house was pulled down, but its name is perpetuated by a row of villas in Tivoli Road, by Meadow Bank Terrace, and by Mr. Heard's dairy in Chapel Road.

On a piece of ground between Darlington and Chapel Roads, known as "Staples Rough", was built a row of houses of somewhat mixed architecture, and the Knight's Hill Wesleyan Church. The growth of Methodism at Norwood is best described by an extract from *Wesleyan Methodism in the Brixton Hill Circuit* compiled by a Committee of the Quarterly meeting in 1898.

There is no record of the introduction of Wesleyan Methodism into Norwood but it is known that the Rev. William Lavers, a supernumerary minister, conducted services there in 1828. The following is an extract from his memoirs:

". . . . one that expressed deep interest in the spiritual welfare of the inhabitants of Norwood. This village in the vicinity of the Metropolis might well excite their sympathy, for its picturesque scenery and pure atmosphere form a strong and melancholy contrast to its spiritual destitution. (!!!) The services of the Church (St. Luke's) with which is connected a National School and of an Independent Chapel which preceded it, have, it is true, dissipated a portion of the moral darkness. . . ."

The Rev. Wm. Lavers first preached in the house of Mrs. Blanchard of Gibson's Hill in August 1828 and after several months' labour succeeded in forming a Society with twenty members. After a time, services were held in a barn in what is now Leigham Court Road. Mr. Lavers and his friend Mr. Elliott then engaged a large room in the Convent which was at that time standing empty. Here they both preached until the place was sold for a Hotel. This Park Hotel is now occupied by the Convent. The services were then carried on for a year or two in tbe house of Mr. Sherrington senior in High Street, Lower Norwood. Mrs. Clark, a lady living opposite, feeling great interest in the work, built a large room at her own expense for the congregation to worship in. This was close to the present "King's Head". (This was the room used by Plymouth Brethren and designated "Cave of Abdullam") In November 1838 the congregation took possession of a chapel of their own in Windsor Road, which is now (1898) occupied by the Primitive Methodists. After some years the congregation outgrew this chapel in Windsor Road and steps were taken to build a larger one. The present site on Knight's Hill was bought and the Chapel erected at a cost of £993. The foundation stone was laid by John Brogden Junior Esq. on August 4th, 1852, and the Chapel was opened for Divine Service by the Rev. Dr. Bunting, June 17th, 1853. The Sunday School was commenced in 1845 in Windsor Road and met there for some time after the Chapel on Knight's Hill was opened. When the Windsor Road Chapel was let to the Primitive Methodists it became necessary to hold the school in the present Chapel. This continued until 1861 when the schoolroom in Eden Road was built. A Day School was commenced in 1860 in a loft over Mr. Bartley Wilson's stable near the corner of Woodcote Place and Chapel Road (Mr. Bartley Wilson's shop was at the corner of Woodcote Place; the stable still stands behind it). One of the children, however, had the misfortune to fall down the ladder and break his leg. This accident led to the erection of the schoolroom in Eden Road and this is now the only Methodist school left in London.

Additions have from time to time been made to the chapel and school:—1866: The chapel gallery was erected. 1872: The large vestry adjoining the chapel was added, and three classrooms were added to the school. 1894: Resolved to enlarge the chapel by lengthening it and adding a chancel as well as a classroom under the chancel, and to lengthen the school and provide additional class room. The estimated cost of the enlargement and renovation was £2,500. This with the addition of an organ made a total indebtedness of £3,000. In 1880 the circuit was divided and the chapel came under the pastoral oversight of Roupell Park Church. I have the beautifully kept account book of this chapel, begun in 1837. The first four pages were left blank with a pencilled suggestion that a brief History of Methodism in Norwood should be written therein. But it was not until 1947 that the extracts I have quoted were copied on to these pages by Mr. William E. Rilstone who was for many years the respected headmaster of the day schools attached to the chapel. Under the Methodist system ministers are appointed for a short term only, so many ministers have served this chapel. The first name in the book is that of the Rev. Guy Mark Pearse in 1864 (his first church and circuit). Other well-known ministers to serve the chapel were the Rev. John Kinnings (his first appointment), and Mr. Josiah Nix, 1884. Among the many devoted members who have served this church are Mr. George Tomlinson and his son-in-law Mr. Grape, Mr. Henry Bristow, Mr. Frederic Griffiths, and that grand old gentleman Mr. William Mustoe. When he died in 1943 at the ripe old age of 93 he held the record as the oldest Sunday School Superintendent in Methodism. He had been connected with the West Norwood Methodist Sunday School for 76 years, for most of that time in charge of the Sunday School and Band of Hope.

Of the Technical Institute I have already written, so we will continue down the hill. Where Rothschild Street now is were the Huguenot's Almshouses, built in Tudor style. There were three large blocks in the shape of a letter "U". The main block facing Knight's Hill had a small turret, and the two side blocks had quaint little staircases half outside the building and half inside. Originally erected by a Society for Aiding Indigent Foreigners, but failing to carry out its beneficient intention, the property was sold to a M. Spartali, a Greek merchant, under whose ownership the tenements remained empty for about 15 years. This gentleman having suffered severe losses, the property, then known as Rothschild Gardens, was placed into the hands of an agent for letting. Eventually however the whole place was pulled down.

At the corner of Rothschild Street stands the Primitive Methodist Chapel. In the dip of Knight's Hill were several little old cottages and shops, some of which remain. The old "Rosemary Branch" was quite different from the present public house, being a little two-storied building, at the back of which were tea and pleasure gardens which joined on to the Tivoli Gardens of the "King's Head" in the High Street. Next to it, where is now the bus garage, stood a similar little shop belonging to Mr. Petty. You can still see one of these little shops at the side of the bus garage. The semi-detached cottage at the side of it was called Ross Cottage, and here lived Mr. Moon, a labourer at Treadwell's Farm. The house of Mr. Boorer, the decorator, at the corner of Ernest Street is another of these original old cottages. Where Ernest Street now meets Knight's Hill stood a grocer's shop, a low-pitched double-fronted place

once kept by a Mr. John Thorn who was clerk and sexton at St. Luke's Church.

The more modern premises of Mr. Heard's dairy stand between Mr. Boorer's house and another of these old cottages which for many years was the West Norwood police station. In the early days Lower Norwood only had two policemen, both of whom lived in Elder Road, Mr. Harding and Mr. Marsh. These old policemen did twelve hours duty a day, one from noon to midnight, the other from midnight to noon next day. On Sundays one policeman would have twenty-four hours off while the other did a twenty-four hour duty in order to change over from night to day. They had a small brick-built sentry box at the corner of High Street and Chapel Road, for Lower Norwood had no police station, the nearest being at Gipsy Hill. If the policeman arrested anyone for a trivial offence the prisoner was often rescued on the fields at the end of Gipsy Road on his way to the station, but if it was for a serious crime the policeman could always rely on plenty of help. Then the cottage in Knight's Hill was taken over, and cells were built on the side of it. Mr. Marsh became the first station sergeant. Eventually this little village police station was closed, whether owing to the abseece of crime or because Norwood's misdeeds remained undiscovered I cannot say, but the district is now back where it used to be with its nearest police station at Gipsy Hill.

Three more old-fashioned shops lying back down a slight slope came next to the police towards Knight's Hill Square. This little turning, once called Soapsuds Square, contained a pretty little colony of very old one-storied cottages, some of brick and others whitewashed. They were some of the oldest property in Norwood, and it was a quaint little backwater. Most of the property in the square, together with the old police station, and the little shops which adjoined it, were destroyed by a flying-bomb in 1944. Two similar little cottages stood between the square and the railway station, also Ivy House, which was displaced by a frontage of shops with a forge at the back of them.

Right opposite Wolfington Road, behind the shops, stood the Public Hall, the centre of entertainment in Norwood. One entered the Public Hall from Knight's Hill, and walked down a long carpeted slope, with palms on either side, into the Hall itself. Many and varied were the entertainments and meetings there in the days before cinemas, gramophones, and wireless. The concerts and amateur dramatic performances were very popular, and in those days it really was "Carriages at half past ten", for a long line of carriages would be drawn up outside the Public Hall. In addition to the "Anomalies" already mentioned, there was the Upper Norwood Amateur Dramatic Society, the Old Lancastrians, and the Ellesmere Dramatic Club who gave a notable performance of *The Prisoner of Zenda*. The Norwood Choral and Orchestral Society under the able baton of Mr. Percy S. Bright, Mus.Bac., F.R.C.O., gave many performances of classical music. Concerts were frequently given at the Public Hall by local residents for various charities. Four brothers of the Mackness family, Arthur, Herbert, Ray and Reg., and a sister, provided the whole programme on several occasions, as also did members of the Baxendale family, Constance, Ruth, Mabel and Christabel. I can well remember the cripple girls from John Groom's Orphanage making artificial flowers in the old Public Hall in aid of their funds, and a play called "On the Line" in aid of the West Norwood Ambulance. I also once made an appearance on the stage there at the end of 1918 in a fine performance of *Romeo and Juliet* by the old scholars of Gipsy Road School. The Public Hall was also the scene of many lively meetings at election times, with Mr. Jim Skitterall as "chucker-out" for the Conservatives: his huge orange rosette could be seen a mile off. The closing of the old Public Hall soon after the war of 1914–18 was a great loss to the neighbourhood, though its flat floor did make it almost impossible for those in the back rows to see the stage properly. It was opened in 1886 by the Lord Mayor of London (in mufti). It has since been used for various commercial purposes.

Another building which has not changed a scrap with the passing years is West Norwood's wooden railway station. It was erected by the same builder and on the same plan as Streatham Hill railway station, and I have been told by an old railway employee there that plans for the improvement of this latter station have been in the station-master's office for upwards of thirty-five years, so there is hope of some improvement for West Norwood some day. An old plan of the district dated 1858 which I possess describes it as the "new station on the West End & Crystal Palace Railway". The line from the Crystal Palace to Wandsworth Common was opened 1st December, 1856. When the station was first built there was a signal-box up high on a level above Knight's Hill by the side of the station nearest to Cotswold Street. This was later replaced by a signal-box on the platform. Old residents remember the large bell on it which was rung by the signalman when a train was approaching. Some of the latecomers would scramble up the bank in Cotswold Street to the platform. This signal-box was done away with on Sunday, 25th March, 1928, and the signal-box at West Norwood Junction by the Lansdowne Hill Bridge now controls the section with modern electrically-worked signals. A small building on each platform served as a waiting-room, and the platforms were uncovered. When Lower Norwood became West Norwood the name board of the station read:

WEST NORWOOD
Change here for Lower Norwood,
Auckland Hill, Beulah Hill,
Crown Hill and the Cemetery.

The early trains were quaint old four-wheeled coaches with oil lamps in the roofs. Pretty little Stroudley tank engines in light brown livery and tall copper-topped chimneys pulled the trains. They were named after stations on the line, Crystal Palace, Anerley, Norwood, etc., but these were discontinued as passengers mistook the names of the engines for the destination of the trains.

In 1910 the London Brighton & South Coast Railway Co. decided to carry out the electrification of the line on the overhead conductor system, using high-tension alternating current at 6,600 volts. A forest of iron girders sprang up to support the overhead wires, and I can well remember the first electric train which ran through West Norwood. This service began regular running from Victoria to the Crystal Palace on the 12th May 1911. In June 1912 the London Bridge section was opened. With the re-grouping of railways, the L.B. & S.C. Rly. was absorbed into the Southern, and it was decided to bring the overhead system into line with the South-Western third rail system. Accordingly the track was converted to direct current at 660 volts, with positive third rail and running rail return. This new service began regular operation between Crystal Palace and Victoria and London Bridge on the 17th June, 1928. Once again I saw the first "third rail" electric train pass through West Norwood.

The line through West Norwood is not a main line, but it does carry a large amount of goods traffic from Willesden Junction to the large depot at Norwood Junction. These goods trains have to negotiate a sharpish "S" bend through West Norwood station and immediately have to face the sharp 1 in 79 incline parallel with Auckland Hill. This bend, coupled with the sudden sharp rise, often causes the couplings on the goods train to break. At times the engines are unable to restart on the steep hill, and I have often seen an electric train assisting by pushing a goods train from the back. Even the steam engines on the goods trains will disappear in time, for in 1941–42 the Southern Railway built an electric locomotive. In February 1942 I received a note from Mr. A. Mitchell, a signalman at Tulse Hill, telling me that the new electric locomotive was making its trial trips with a train of eleven coaches on Tuesday and Wednesday the 17th and 18th of February, passing through West Norwood between 11 and 11.5 a.m., so thanks to Mr. Mitchell I can say that I saw all the three types of electric traction making their first trial trips through West Norwood station.

To complete our survey of Knight's Hill we must now retrace out steps to the present Brotherhood buildings. The house that is now the Brotherhood Institute was once occupied by a Dr. Austin. Then after the war of 1914–18 it became the Lambeth Borough Maternity Home before it moved to the premises higher up the hill. That live organisation, the West Norwood Brotherhood, began at the Congregational Chapel in Chapel Road, the Institute being at Canton Villa, Windsor Grove. In 1927, the church needing more accommodation for its Sunday School, the Brotherhood committee purchased the premises on Knight's Hill, and commenced to build the splendid hall at the side of it. This hall was opened on Saturday the 1st September, 1928, by H.R.H. Princess Louise, and a great work has been carried on there ever since. For many years the annual Brotherhood Pantomime has been an event of the year, and has always been of a very high standard, even under wartime conditions.

Among the local gentlemen who have been prominent in the West Norwood Brotherhood are Messrs. N. W. Hubbard, J.P., F. D. Lapthorn, J.P., one-time National President of the Brotherhood movement; John Day, J.P.; R. L. Martin; and many others, including Mr. James Barfoot, for many years the honorary secretary, who will also be remembered as the Borough Council's sanitary inspector in this district. The Brotherhood have always had a fine orchestra, and the West Norwood Sisterhood is an equally fine organisation whose meetings are held in the Brotherhood Hall every week. Among those who have played their part in the success of the Sisterhood are Miss Hubbard, Mrs. Ballinger, Mrs. Barfoot and Mrs. Vince. Both the Brotherhood and Sisterhood have done great benevolent work in West Norwood.

Between Thornlaw Road and St. Julian's Farm Road stood a large building, something like a huge barn, which was used for temporary services while the roof of St. Luke's Church was being rebuilt in 1870.

Where the Royal Cinema now stands stood the premises of Mr. Crittal, a butcher. The cinema, opened about the year 1909–10, was the first "Picture Palace" in Norwood. The children's matinée on Saturday afternoons has always been very popular, and I have vivid recollections of how we all cheered and booed in the days of Pearl White and Arnold Daly in the serial "The Exploits of Elaine", each exciting instalment ending with a large question-mark on which was imposed the all-important question—"Who is the Clutching Hand???" How we laughed at Pimple and Tweedledum and Tweedledee long before we were to laugh at Charlie Chaplin and Walt Disney.

Between Wolfington Road and the railway the only house was Wolfington House School kept by Mr. and Mrs. Compton. They afterwards moved the school to Lancaster Road where it became Lancaster College. Mr. Osman Thomas afterwards became headmaster, and the school was eventually moved to Tulse Hill.

By the side of the railway stood the very handsome gates of the Jews' Orphanage. The gates were removed when owing to a fire at the orphanage it was found that there was not sufficient room for a fire engine to pass in. The Jews' Hospital and Orphanage is one of the oldest charitable institutions of Jews in England. The founders were B. & A. Goldsmid, and it was originally established in Mile End in 1806. In 1861 Mr. Barnet Meyers who owned property in Norwood presented the hospital with nine and a half acres of freehold land on Knight's Hill. The foundation stone was laid by Sir Anthony Rothschild on June 6th, 1861. The building, constructed of brick with stone dressings, in the Jacobean style, was completed in 1863 from the designs of Mr. Tillot. The buildings include a small synagogue and school workshops erected at a cost of £700 furnished by Mr. B. L. Cohen. A further addition to the main buildings was the Arnold and Jane Gabriel Homes with frontage to Wolfington Road. During the war of 1939–45 the children were evacuated, and the buildings were used as a training college by the National Fire Service.

Where the railway line is now stood the original "Horns Tavern". This is the oldest public house in Norwood, and is marked on Rocque's map of 1746 and on all succeeding maps. The original building was an old timber-built hostelry which was pulled down when the railway came. A new building was erected at the side of the railway, and this in turn was pulled down in 1937 to make way for the larger modern public house which stands there now. When George III came to the throne in 1760 the "Horns" was kept by a retired coachman named John Catley. His name would have been forgotten but for his daughter, then 15. Having displayed early talent she was put into training, and became one of the most famous singers and actresses of her day. She took London by storm, women copied her style of hair-dressing, and famous men sought her companion-ship. She made her first appearance at Vauxhall Gardens in 1762, and in 1769 she was singing in Dublin where she made the acquaintance of O'Keefe the dramatist, then a young man of 18. In his reminiscences O'Keefe has left an interesting description of her. He says

"She wore her hair plain over her forehead in an even line almost to her eyebrows, and the word was with all the ladies to have their hair 'Catleyfied'. Miss Catley and her oddities were well-known to all. She was one of the most beautiful women I ever saw, the expression of her eyes, and the smiles and dimples that played around her lips and cheeks, enchanting. She was eccentric but had an excellent heart,'

Anne Catley married General Lascelles, whom William Mason once described as "a strutting carrion crow" and she died at his house at Brentford on the 14th of October 1789. There is a book in the British Museum Library called *The Life of Anne Catley*, by Miss Ambross, written in 1790.

Between the "Horns" and the bottom of Knight's Hill stood an old house lying back, with well-wooded gardens in front, called Elm Cottage. It was I believe originally the parsonage. There is a picture of this house in the Public Library. Mr. Nettlefold of Streatham bought the site and presented sufficient of it to Lambeth for the erection of the Public Library which was opened in 1888 at a total cost of £4,500. The name Nettlefold Place commemorates this gift of land. The West Norwood Library was enlarged in 1936. Next to the library is the West Norwood Sorting Office. Before the railings of St. Luke's Church were set back there was a notice fixed to them at the bottom of the hill which read: "Please slacken your horse's bearing rein before climbing the hill." We have now walked round in a big circle, and come back to our starting point at the fountain. To continue our journey we will go back a little to Hannen Road and Auckland Hill.

33

34

35

36

37

38

39

40

41

42

43

44

45

46

47

48

Chapter 15
Hannen Road and Auckland Hill

Hannen Road is named after Mr. James Hannan, a Judge of the High Court, who was buried at Norwood Cemetery in 1894. At the top of Hannen Road, once called St. Luke's Villas, was the cab rank on which stood the four-wheeled cabs. The cabmen's shelter still stands there although the old horse cabs have long disappeared. Mr. Chamberlain and Mr. Olly Mitchell were two well-known cabmen on this rank. West Norwood station occupies the whole of one side of the road while on the other side are a few shops and then some large old houses, the last one of which, Hannen House, has been the Borough Council Welfare Centre and Clinic for many years.

Crossing High Street we come into Auckland Hill. This road is now completely built on, but little more than 50 years ago there were only a few large houses, in between which were open spaces covered with ballast left from old brickmaking days. The ballast was used to make up the road, giving it a red appearance, and Auckland Hill was known locally as the Red Hill. I remember during a heavy snowfall in 1940 seeing men digging up the road to get at a burst water main. The old red ballast which they dug out was then strikingly noticeable against the white snow. On the left as we enter Auckland Hill is the Auckland Hall Evangelical Church, founded and built by Mr. T. W. Stoughton of the book publishing firm of Hodder and Stoughton. He lived at Hanbury Villa, Gypsy Road, before moving to Beulah Hill. Next to the Hall is Auckland Flats, a tall rather odd and isolated building, at the side and back of which was the little colony of cottages called Auckland Place. Most of these small cottages, which were often flooded in times gone by as they were over the Effra, were pulled down under the L.C.C.'s clearance scheme in 1938.

From Auckland Place an old, now disused road called Pilgrim Hill ran up the line of the cemetery wall, coming out into Auckland Hill again at the top of the hill. This road led up to an entrance of the cemetery, but the entrance was closed and the road discarded by the cemetery company. The gardens of the houses on the left hand side of Auckland Hill now cover this old road except for a few yards, at the bottom end. Here stand three very old detached houses; the first is Mr. Minter's, the stonemason's, and the last has been for many years The Retreat, a private maternity home run by Nurse Q. Simpson. Some large old houses stand at the corner of the present Hubbard Road which was the top end of the original Pilgrim Hill. At the end of Hubbard Road were some gates to the cemetery, now bricked up. On the right-hand side of Hubbard Road is the West Norwood Crèche.

Some years ago a baby was burned to death when left in charge of another child while the mother was out at work. This tragedy so distressed Mrs. Donald Campbell that she enlisted the help of Dr. Harris and other friends to open a Crèche or day nursery where babies and infants are taken care of and fed while the mothers are at work. Upon the death of Dr. Harris, Dr. Welch became honorary medical adviser to the Crèche, and Mrs. Welch remained chairman of the committee of ladies until well past her 94th birthday. This good work has from the start been carried on voluntarily without any state or municipal aid. By the side of the Crèche, lying back in a long front garden, stood a large old house called Auckland House. This was once the residence of a Mr. Eden who was, I believe, dentist to Queen Victoria. The house was demolished by a bomb in 1940.

The right-hand side of Auckland Hill from High Street consists almost entirely of tall old houses with the flats known locally as Wheeler's sandwiched between them. At the very end of that side of Auckland Hill nearest to Gipsy Road stands little Willow Cottage, the residence of Mr. Welham, the builder. From Hubbard Road to St. Louis Road was Mr. Welham's orchard. At the corner of St. Louis Road stands the Reform Club, described, when it was first built by Mr. Ben Bristow, the builder, as the finest set of club premises in South London. The waste ground bounded by St. Cloud Road, St. Gothard Road and St. Louis Road was known locally as "No man's land." It was on this piece of ground that Lord George Sanger erected the marquee and sideshows of his circus, an annual event much looked forward to. At the corner of St. Cloud and St. Gothard Roads stood a tumbledown old cottage, occupied by Mr. Benton a nurseryman, before he removed to the present Benton's Lane. About 1859 it was occupied by Mr. and Mrs. E. Avis. The old cottage, which belonged to Mr. Eden, had a gate made out of farm implements.

St. Gothard Road was formerly called Elder Lane. In St. Louis Road was the little Providence Strict Baptist Chapel, with the minister's house, Providence Cottage, at the side of it. The Rev. Harry Patterson was the well-respected minister here for many years. The building was demolished by a flying-bomb in 1944. At the bottom of St. Cloud Road, in what looks like a short extension of St. Gothard Road, stands a quaint little dwelling called The Lodge. St. Cloud Road runs down into Rommany Road, that end of this road being once called Dagmar Road. The "Dagmar Arms" was a public house which stood at the corner facing the present Hamilton Grove. At the far end of Dagmar Road by the back of Emmanuel Hall was Marshall's pottery, where roof tiles and red chimney-pots were made. It is now the Borough Council's road maintenance depot. A small hall called St. Louis Hall stood back in St. Louis Road between St. Gothard Road and Rommany Road, and close by in Rommany Road itself is the Scott Memorial Hall belonging to the London City Mission. All the area which is now Rommany Road, Hamilton Road and Clive Road was a swampy flat stretching towards Dulwich, with a mere footpath following the line of the present Gipsy Road. This swampy flat together with the common land on the right-hand side of Gipsy Hill was the habitation of gipsies.

Chapter 16
The Gipsies

The date of the first appearance of the gipsies in Norwood is doubtful, but the history of this well-known encampment certainly goes back a long way and is commemorated by such names as Gipsy Road, Gipsy Hill, the Gipsy Queen, the Gipsy House, and Rommany Road. A row of houses in Gipsy Road was also named Zingari Terrace. As far back as 1668 the gipsy encampment was well established in Norwood, for in the famous diary of Samuel Pepys is the following entry for August 11th 1668:

"This afternoon my wife and Mercer and Deb went with Pelling to see the gypsies at Lambeth, and have their fortunes told; but what they did, I did not enquire."

A footnote to Bright's edition of the diary says: "Most probably at Norwood."

The most famous of all the gipsies was Margaret Finch described as the "original Queen of the Norwood Gipsies." Her fame spread throughout the surrounding districts, and she was visited by great numbers. She died in 1740 at the ripe old age of 108, and was buried on the 24th October in Beckenham Parish Church. It is said that she remained for so long in a squatting position that when she died her limbs could not be straightened, and it was necessary to bury her in a deep square box. I have an old drawing of her presented to me by Mr. Henry Bristow, who called his house 103, Gipsy Hill "Queenwood," for it was said that Margaret Finch used to sit under a large old tree in his garden. She was succeeded by her niece, "Queen Bridget" who died in 1768, and lies buried in the old graveyard at Dulwich.

The "Gipsy House" wrote Lysons about 1790 "is situated on a small green in a valley surrounded by woods. On this ground a few families of gipsies have pitched their tents for a great number of years." The map in Allen's *History of Lambeth* (1825) shows the "Gipsy House" as being situated just about where Mr. Bristow's house stands, near the corner of Oaks Avenue in Gipsy Hill. Another old drawing shows that there were one or two little wooden shacks occupied by gipsies in this area.

In 1777 a pantomime "The Norwood Gypsies" was produced at Covent Garden. A copy of the airs and duets is at the British Museum. The gipsies disappeared after the Enclosure Act of 1797 when the common land was enclosed and the police broke up the encampment.

Chapter 17
Gipsy Road

Entering Gipsy Road from the High Street on the left-hand side are first two shops, one double-fronted and one very small. By the side of the latter is the entrance to the little Victoria Hall which has been used for various purposes. Next come two pairs of old semi-detached houses, between which a modern block of flats has been squeezed. The first pair are charming old houses, and the second pair were rather tall severe-looking houses. In the first of these lived the charming North family for many years. Mr. Francis North and his two sisters were perfect examples of Victorian gentlefolks, and they were greatly respected in the neighbourhood. They all lived to a great age. Mr. North once told me that his first recollection of Norwood as a small boy was of his mother buying the linoleum for the house at my great-grandfather's shop. Old Mrs. North was of Spanish birth, and had ten christian names. The house next door was occupied for many years by Miss Margaret Muir and her aunt Miss Elvira Leslie, both well-known teachers of music. Miss Leslie was in her day a noted pianist and elocutionist, having studied under Leybach in Toulon and Sir Julius Benedict at the Royal Academy of Music.

Then comes a terrace of houses to the present Gipsy Road School. Where the school now stands was a smallholding and orchard on which stood a rough wooden squatter's hut where lived Mr. Hollis. He was an irascible old man, probably because the boys who "went scrumping" in his orchard would shout "Monkey" Hollis after him because of his simian features. When he died the people who held the title-deeds of the ground took possession of it. His son took this to heart and became a man with a grievance, making periodical appearances at the courts. When his little hut was pulled down a large crowd gathered in anticipation of some fun. It was pulled down by Mr. Abbott, the house-breaker in Chapel Road, who, so I have read, came well primed for the occasion, and harangued the crowd from the roof.

Gipsy Road School was carried on from 1872 to 1875 in a temporary iron building. The transfer from the British School to Board School took place in May 1872. Mr. Charles Wilson the headmaster from the British School in Chapel Road became the first headmaster, and Mrs. Selby was the headmistress of the girls' school. In 1875 the school was opened in the permanent building, the average attendance in the boys' school being 330. The total attendance was nearly 1,400. The school has been altered and enlarged once or twice since then. This school was the first one my father attended. His teacher was Mr. Chatwin, whose wife was the headmistress of the Junior Mixed School when I went there. Mr. Chatwin was killed in a cycling accident in 1909. It occurs to me that the teachers there must hold something of a record for long service at the school, for some of the masters, Mr. Brereton Senr., Mr. Routledge, Mr. Taylour, and Mr. Duncan, who taught my father, were still there when I went there. When my son went to the school there were Mr. Brereton junior, Miss Brereton, Mr. Jones, Mr. Rollasson, and Miss Bassett who were teachers there in my time. The school has always held a good record for football and cricket.

There is a small school attached to it for mentally defective children.

On the right-hand side of Gipsy Road the garden of Clifton Lodge reached down to an old house, demolished by a bomb in 1940, called The Hollies. This was the residence of the Price family, the makers of candles. After the war of 1914–18, it became the Edith Cavell Home of Rest for Nurses, being one of two such homes purchased from the Nurse Cavell Memorial Fund. The gardens of Clifton Lodge are now covered with a short road, and new permanent pre-fabricated houses of a special type have been built there since the war of 1939–45. As I write all the remaining property on this side of Gipsy Road (with the exception of the block of flats called Elder Gardens) is about to be demolished up to the railway bridge, including all the remaining houses in Benton's Lane. This property includes, starting from Elder Gardens, first a row of villas to the corner of Benton's Lane, behind which is an old house standing in a large garden, Wildwood House, approached through a gateway. Benton's Lane, once called Hollis Lane, had some very old houses on the left side, including some timber-built cottages. The right-hand side had no houses at all until the more modern Gladstone Terrace was built. Then from the corner of Benton's Lane to the railway bridge were first, two shops, then three private houses lying back a bit with front gardens. One of these was a private school which my grandfather attended, known as "Cocky" Kendall's school. Next to these houses was a little pathway, so narrow as to be almost unnoticed by passers-by, which led down to a colony of very old dwellings called Lepine Cottages. This quaint little backwater of Norwood was a charming spot, and might well have been in the heart of the country. All these cottages were destroyed by a flying bomb in 1944, and this area is about to be developed as a housing estate by the Borough Council. At the top of the rise by the corner of Auckland Hill stands the "Gipsy House" public house. The present building, damaged in the bombing close by, replaced a former building the entrance to which was down a few steps. It was named after an earlier "Gipsy House" at the foot of Gipsy Hill half a mile away. Next door to this present Gipsy House stood the "tin tabernacle" where the Rev. Walter Hobbs conducted his ministry. I will refer to this later. After this iron building was pulled down a nursery school was erected on the site. This was destroyed by a flying bomb. From this point to the Paxton Hotel, this side of Gipsy Road, which was once flat and swampy ground, has not altered a great deal in the past 60 years. The other side of the road from the railway to Salter's Hill School was rough ground until the row of small flats was built. Salter's Hill School was carried on about 1878 in an iron building in Rommany Road. Three years later it was moved to the present site. This school has a handicrafts centre for woodwork, laundry, and cookery. Salter's Hill was once called Hamilton Hill after Mr. Hamilton who lived at Bloomfield Hall. All the right-hand side is bounded by Norwood Park except for a pair of tall houses, one of which, named Haddon, was the residence of the Rev. Walter Hobbs. Above these houses there used to stand the residence of a family named Nicholls, and opposite the corner of Bloomhall Road were one or two small shacks. Where Oaks Avenue is now was an estate called The Oaks. It had a frontage to Gipsy Road and Gipsy Hill.

The Baptist Church in Gipsy Road originated in 1873 when services were held at the Paxton school-room, Clive Road. The Rev. Walter Hobbs became pastor in November 1880, and on the 27th September 1881 the foundation stone of the new church in Gipsy Road was laid by Mr. Horace B. Marshall, F.R.G.S. The builders of the church were Messrs. J. Smith & Sons of South Norwood. On the 9th January 1882 Mr. Marshall's son, Mr. Horace E. B. Marshall (subsequently Lord Mayor of London) laid the top stone of the building. The new chapel, which held 700 people, had an open-timbered roof, with circular platform and galleries. The nature of the site permitted a lofty schoolroom seating 500. The style of architecture is Early English. The actual opening of the church took place on Tuesday the 16th May 1882. The total outlay was £4,700. The first Sunday services were conducted by the Rev. John Spurgeon, father of the Rev. Charles H. Spurgeon.

Under the pastorate of the Rev. Walter Hobbs the work prospered, and additional class rooms were added to the building in 1890. An organ was built in the chapel in 1887 at a cost of £750, and the world-famous organist, Alfred Hollins, gave the opening recital.

The Rev. W. Hobbs also did good work on the Board of Guardians. He represented the Norwood Ward of Lambeth Parish, from 1888 to 1910. Mr. Hobbs took particular interest in the children at the Lambeth Schools in Elder Road, where he was chairman of the Schools Committee. He claimed to have brought about the following changes – The attendance of the children at the Public Elementary Schools, thus raising the standard from the lower grade of Poor Law education. The removal of the workhouse stigma by the children not having a uniform dress. Their Sunday School which commenced in 1895. Also a Band of Hope. He also arranged for them to have an annual day at the seaside.

Eventually there was some dissension among the church members, some of whom thought that Mr. Hobbs was devoting too much of his time to his work as Guardian of the poor. Finally Mr. Hobbs resigned the pastorate in December 1898. A public testimonial was set on foot, and in January 1899 in the West Norwood Institute a purse of £157 was presented to Mr. Hobbs.

Within a week pressure was brought to bear on him to continue his work in West Norwood. Services were commenced in the Welcome Hall, Westow Street, and a church was formed with a membership of 137. Later a site was secured in Gipsy Road and an iron building seating 450 persons was erected at a total cost of £900 which was opened the first week in 1901. Here Mr. Hobbs continued his ministry until he died in 1914. This iron building, called The Tabernacle, was erected next door to the "Gipsy House". An old white-washed cottage called Rose Cottage previously stood on the site. It was used as a laundry and the washing was hung out to dry on the waste ground at the back of it. The life story of the Rev. Walter Hobbs, *Pastor and Guardian* by John Stuart, was published by Arthur H. Stockwell, of 29 Ludgate Hill.

At the end of Gipsy Road we come to the Paxton Hotel, named after Sir Joseph Paxton, the designer and builder of the Crystal Palace. Its present landlord is the old Surrey cricketer Ernie Hayes. At the side of the Paxton Hotel is the Paxton Yard where Messrs. Thomas Tilling had their stabling.

Chapter 18
West Dulwich

The History of Dulwich has already been written by Edwin T. Hall, Allan M. Galer, and other writers, but parts of the district are so closely connected with West Norwood that I must include some of it.

Let us take Rosendale Road first, that lovely wide straight road that seems to lead straight to Big Ben as you walk down it from the Tritton Road end. This end of the road contains some blocks of flats of somewhat odd architectural styles all mixed up with modern red brick houses. At the corner of Park Hall Road stands the new Gipsy Hill automatic telephone exchange. Telephones in West Norwood were transferred from the manually operated Streatham exchange to the automatic Gipsy Hill exchange in December 1939. Tritton Road was formerly called Paget Road, the principal building being the Emmanuel Hall, the parish hall of Emmanuel Church. In small premises in the corner of Tritton and Martell Roads the Telephone Manufacturing Company first began business. Their large factory, called Hollingsworth Works, now dominates Martell Road. This large concern also has branches on Auckland Hill and on Knight's Hill. At the corner of Myton Road and Martell Road was Mr. Dickenson's photographic studio, and between Myton Road and Park Road in Martell Road stands a tiny iron chapel used by the Plymouth Brethren. The Rosendale Hotel stands on the opposite corner to the telephone exchange. At the back of the hotel is the bowling green of the Northwood Bowling Club. At the side of the hotel are two very small shops, one a tobacconist's, and the other the little hairdresser's shop of Mr. Hymus. Then is an old house with a yard at the side where Mr. Charles Sills had a jobmaster's business. Then a row of old houses to the corner of Idmiston Road, at the Rosendale Road end of which are some small old houses, to Chancellor Grove. This part of Idmiston Road was formerly called Buccleugh Road. There are some old established businesses in the row of shops between Idmiston and Eastmearn Roads, among them Wakefield's, grocer; Peter's, bootmaker; Marden, stationer; Wood, butcher; and Dale, boot repairer. On the opposite side of the road from Park Road to Carson Road are some large old houses between which is a short cul-de-sac called Elmworth Grove, consisting of one or two small cottages badly damaged by bombing in 1944. All Saints Church in Rosendale Road is a fine building erected about 50 years ago. At the Lovelace Road end of the church provision was made for further extension. The first vicar was the Rev. James Beeby, M.A., who had been one of the clergy at St. Peter's, Leigham Court Road. Upon Mr. Beeby's death the Rev. Gordon Ward was vicar and he too died in office. He was succeeded by the Rev. C. Patteson, M.A., and he in turn by the present vicar

the Rev. J. Capron. The interior of the church is very beautiful and contains a magnificent font. For many years the talented Mr. F. W. Holloway, F.R.C.O., the organist at the Crystal Palace, was organist and choirmaster at this church. Owing to bomb damage, services are at the moment held in the crypt.

At the corner of Turney Road is the Rosendale Road School, and on the other side of the road is the large coal wharf which belonged to the London Midland & Scottish Railway Company. Thurlow Park Road has always been a high class residential road, and it contains some fine large houses. At the Tulse Hill end on the right-hand side is Westbank School for Girls. Miss Jones is the principal. At the corner of Elmcourt Road is St. Cuthbert's Presbyterian Church of England, which began in a temporary iron church erected on the site of what was Keeler's Nursery. The Rev. Robert Taylor conducted the inaugural service. The fine new church was then built on the site, the Rev. Wm. Armstrong being its first minister. Other ministers were the Rev. Hay Colligan, the Rev. Wm. Buckingham, and the Rev. E. A. Taylor-Davies who died in office in 1941. At the back of Thurlow Park Road on the other side is "The Birkbeck", a triangle of roads formed by Birkbeck Hill and Place and Thurlow Hill. The Dulwich High School for Girls stands at the junction of Thurlow Park Road and Lancaster Avenue. On the other side of the road at No. 101, Thurlow Park Road, lived Dr. Wm. B. Robertson whose five sons all practised in the district, John and James in Christchurch Road, and William and George in Thurlow Park Road. A few yards along at No. 107 lived Mr. John Pearce whose career as a caterer made a romantic story. The names Pearce and Plenty were as well known as the meat puddings, called "four-penny-busters" which was a speciality at their restaurants. Mr. Pearce was the founder of the J.P. Restaurants. Another notable resident of Thurlow Park Road was the Rt. Hon. J. H. Thomas, M.P., who lived at No. 125.

The shopping centre at the crossroads of Croxted Road and Park Hall Road suffered severely from successive flying-bombs in 1944. Old tradesmen here were: Buckle, grocer; H. A. Mills, chemist; H. J. Watford, confectioner; and Ashley and Wright's dairy in Croxted Road and Paddles, nursery; Lydall & Son, printers; Collins, fruiterer; Hutchinson, draper; J. T. Moss & Son, builders; French, baker; Francis, draper; Barnes, cycles; G. King, tailor; Slade, hairdresser in Park Hall Road.

In Clive Road is Emmanuel Church built in 1877. The old vicarage stood where the block of flats called Clevedon Court now stands. The new vicarage at the corner of Chalford Road was erected just before the war of 1939–45. The Rev. Eben Rae, M.A., was vicar for many years until his death. The Rev. T. G. Edwards, the present vicar of Holy Trinity, succeeded him.

In Carnac Street is the West Norwood Central School built nearly twenty years ago. Opposite the school is a public house the "Bricklayer's Arms". Both Hamilton and Clive Roads consist of small fairly old houses. In the corner of Hamilton Road, between this road and Rommany Road, are the pretty little St. Saviour's College Almshouses. The following inscription in the old almshouses speaks for itself:

ST. SAVIOUR'S SOUTHWARK.

The various almshouses and the Chapel within this ground were erected in the years 1862 & 1863 during the Wardenship (for 2 years) of James Newton (Great Account), Robert Tiffin (Renter), John Henry Muller (College), George Mansell (Bell), Charles Dyer Field (Newcomers), Benjamin Kedgley (Young, Spratt & Jacksons).

The first stone laid by

John Henry Muller, the College Warden, on the 9th October 1862.

They were rebuilt on this ground in consequence of the site of the College and Ground in the Parish of St. Saviour, Southwark, whereon they were originally erected and stood having been taken for the purposes of the Charing Cross Railway.

Edward Habershon, Architect.

Herbert Sturmy, Vestry Clerk.

These almshouses, with the lovely quadrangle and fine gates, are an ornament to the neighbourhood. They were damaged, but not too badly, by a flying-bomb which demolished the houses next to them and also badly damaged the Hamilton Road Methodist Church. The present Warden of St. Saviour's College is the genial Mr. A. E. Hobbs whose father was Warden before him.

At the corner of Clive Road and Hamilton Road stood a public house called the "Hamilton Arms", closed under the Redundancy Act in 1935, and demolished in 1938 to make way for a modern block of flats. Another little public house in Hamilton Road is the "Crown", nicknamed the "Bug and Bolster". Mr. J. Newton was the landlord for many years. Some of the older tradesmen in the shops in this part of Hamilton Road are: Bennett, greengrocer; Godfrey, newsagent; W. March, oil and colour; Bedford, wardrobe dealer; Wheeler, butcher; Norris, greengrocer; and Miss Botting, laundry. On the other side: Collier, baker; Gale, grocer; Palmer, hairdresser; Croft, draper; and A. Gillett, plumber. Two little backwaters of Hamilton Road are Surrey Mews and Paxton Yard.

Chapter 19
Gipsy Hill and Westow Hill

At the bottom of Gipsy Hill is the field between Gipsy Hill and The Avenue known as French's Field, where cows used to graze. It was the last place in Norwood where I saw cows driven through the streets. At each end of this field are two small triangular plots, one beside the Paxton Hotel at the meeting of the roads, and the other where The Avenue joins Gipsy Hill. These two plots are said to be old plague pits but although this has been handed down for generations there is nothing to substantiate it. On an old map of Camberwell the two plots were marked on the very edge of Camberwell parish, and it seems feasible that if they are plague pits that they should be dug at the extremity of the parish. It may be that the idea that they were plague pits arose from Defoe's book *The Journal of the Plague Year* in which he refers to victims of the plague being found among the woods and commons at Norwood. For the whole of the right-hand side of Gipsy Hill was Norwood Common, and Rocque's map shows that one or two tracks through the woods met at this point. Defoe's book goes on to describe the burial of these poor folk: "Who", he says:

> "wandered away and died in the outlying districts. . . . The number of these miserable objects was great. The country people would go and dig a hole at a distance from them and then with long poles with hooks at the end of them, drag the bodies into these pits and then throw the earth in from as far as they could caste it to cover them."

There was too a large encampment of gipsies on Norwood Common near this site, and we can assume thay they were not immune from the plague and that many of them died of it. So much for the evidence in favour; now for the evidence against.

Walter G. Bell in his book "Unknown London" published in 1920, writing on page 213 of the Great Plague, says:

> "The world knows that time of horror only from Defoe's 'Journal of the Plague Year', a work that owes its apparent authenticity to the author's art alone, assisted by copious quotations from printed and manuscript records at his hand. Much unprofitable ingenuity has been spent in seeking to establish that the 'H.F.' the reputed writer of the 'Journal' was Defoe's uncle, Henry Foe. The book was given to the world as fiction."

We must also remember that at the time of the plague London did not stretch further south than Southwark, a long way from Gipsy Hill, and too far for the death carts to have come even if there had been good roads. There is another triangular plot opposite Ruskin Park on Denmark Hill that is also said to have been a plague pit.

The Avenue and the lower end of Gipsy Hill both have some fine large houses, one of which, Queenswood, I have already mentioned. At a house called Sunnyside on Gipsy Hill, Mrs. Henry Wood, the author of *East Lynne*, lived for many years. Gipsy Hill was originally called King William IV Hill after a little public house which stood close by the corner of Woodland Road. Two tiny cottages with rooms on the ground floor only kept the public house company. One was tenanted by a Mrs. Lee, said to be the last of the Norwood gipsies. The public house was closed under the Act of 1935. Gipsy Hill railway station is a nice red brick building far superior in style to the wooden shed which does duty for a station at West Norwood. The first Christ Church on Gipsy Hill was an iron building erected in 1862. The foundation stone of the present fine church building was laid on the 12th July, 1866, and the consecration ceremony took place on the 8th June, 1867, being conducted by Bishop Sumner of Winchester. The church cost about £16,000. The first vicar was the Rev. R. Allen, M.A., who died 19th February, 1895. He was succeeded by the Rev. R. C. Joynt, M.A., who came from Sheffield. Canon C. E. Wilson, M.A., B.D., who has recently retired, was the greatly respected vicar for many years. The church has accommodation for 1,100, and contains a beautiful organ by Walker & Sons, erected in 1898 at a cost of £1,100. The church has a mission, St. Jude's, in Berridge Road.

Brickfields covered the site of the present Camden Hill Road area and belonged to a Mr. Corner, while Mr. Coles's brickfield was near the site of the High Level station. Cawnpore Street had the doubtful distinction of receiving the first bomb dropped in the London area in the war of 1939–45. Between Camden Hill Road and Westow Hill stands the old Gipsy Hill police station. In the early days there was only one policeman in Upper Norwood: he came from Camberwell. A windmill used to stand at the top of Gipsy Hill at this point, with the Windmill Tea Gardens at the side of it. The windmill was kept by a miller named Paddy who occupied the mill-house close by. The windmill was stopped in 1853, and was pulled down soon afterwards. There is an old story (told in other districts as well) that it was proposed to build a second windmill here but it was not built as the general opinion was that there would not be enough wind to work two.

Turning from Gipsy Hill into Westow Hill and passing the shops we come to the Wesleyan Church, at the side of which are Princess Cottages. The Wesleyan Church was opened in 1874, and will seat 1,000. Many of the most eminent ministers of Methodism have at different times conducted services in the church. The home of Mr. Prime, the veterinary surgeon, next door to the church, is a very old house called Elim Lodge. The Holborn Bars, the old-fashioned wine shop next door, is on the site of a public house called the "Queen's Arms". Further along was the Upper Norwood National School. In 1907 this old building was used by Mr. Morter as a stable. In the days when candles were used for lighting a Mr. Bridge had a candle factory in Westow Hill. The Upper Norwood Library at the corner of Beardell Street, opened in 1895, is administered jointly by Croydon and Lambeth Boroughs. The junior library and lecture hall built in 1936, was opened by A. E. W. Mason, the author.

Opposite the library was a small public house, the "Royal Albert", rebuilt further back from the roadway just before the war of 1939–45. A few yards further on is Upper Norwood's oldest public house, the "Woodman". The old building was very different from the present one. It was an old-fashioned country inn standing back 20 to 30 yards from the street, with a drive and a horse trough in front. I have already mentioned the old sign with the Woodman and his dog painted on it. A block of stone steps used by equestrians to mount their horses stood by the inn door. The doorstep is said to have been on a level with the cross on top of St. Paul's Cathedral. At the side was an ornamental gateway leading to a tea garden and two skittle grounds, one reserved for gentlefolks. It was the chief posting house for the four-in-hands. A coach called "The Gipsy Queen" ran daily from the "Woodman" to the "Greenman and Still" in Oxford Street.

Where St. Aubyns Road is now stood St. Aubyns School, founded in 1812, and kept by Mr. Frederick George Aubin for poor children. Where St. Aubyns church is now was a large model ship fully rigged on which the boys were trained for the sea. Once a month, on Thursdays, the boys in sailor suits manned the rigging and sang "God Save the Queen." They had an old cannon fired once or twice a year which once blew the fence down. The school removed soon after the Crystal Palace was built.

Nearly opposite to St. Aubyns Road was the old Electra Picture Palace. Part of the premises are now used by the Religious Film Library and Studio.

The "White Swan Hotel" at the corner of the Crystal Palace Parade is, like the "Woodman", very different from the old "White Swan". The original inn was built on the site of a smithy kept by a Mr. Adams, within a few yards of the Vicar's Oak. So this story has completed a full circle, for it began with records of the Vicar's Oak and after much rambling we have now come back to it.

The spot where the old tree stood in quiet woodlands is now one of the busiest corners in the district, with a constant flow of traffic of all kinds round the roundabout. The old trams, which my grandfather said would never climb the steep Anerley Hill, have disappeared, and have been replaced by modern trolley-buses.

Even the old Crystal Palace has gone. For over 80 years this huge iron and glass palace had stood on the hill, like a Victorian lady with her crinoline spread out around her, looking down on Norwood.

Old Norwood residents have pleasant memories of the old building and of the many fêtes and functions which took place there, and they all had a lump in their throats as they saw, the night of the 30th of November 1936, the fire which destroyed it, probably the greatest sight that Norwood has ever seen.

Chapter 20
Cavalcade

Having journeyed round the roads and streets of the district we will now in conclusion look back over various items of interest in the past, starting with elections in Norwood. Before the passing of the Reform and Redistribution Acts of 1884–5, Norwood formed part of the East Surrey division, and the last two Conservative members were Messrs Watney and Grantham, the former being connected with the brewing firm, while the latter became Mr. Justice Grantham. Prior to 1883, the year the Corrupt Practices Act was passed, there was no restriction on elections, and all descriptions of vehicles could be hired for election day. Drink flowed in all directions, and it was necessary to have "chuckers-out" at all meetings. Feeling ran very high and often fights took place, but all ended in good feeling as there were large sums of money available for any or all purposes. You can read of the "goings-on" at the old elections in Mr. George Hill's book, *Electoral History of the Borough of Lambeth*. The election of 1857 when William Roupell was elected was the cause of an inquiry at which it was disclosed that Roupell had spent over £5,000 on his election.

When Norwood returned a member of its own, Mr. Thomas Lynn Bristowe, of Denmark Hill, a genial Conservative, was its first M.P. His death at the opening ceremony of Brockwell Park has already been mentioned. Mr. Charles Ernest Tritton was the next member. His family had been closely connected with Norwood by residence at Bloomfield, Central Hill. His father, Mr. Joseph Tritton, was a member of the banking firm of Barclay. He was a prominent Baptist, and was the author of the well-known hymn "Head of the Church and Lord of all." Mr. Charles E. Tritton had a baronetcy bestowed upon him for great public services soon after he was returned member for Norwood, and he was the most popular member Norwood has ever had. In 1906 Sir Ernest, an ardent Free Trader, could not see eye to eye with the Conservative Party in Norwood on the question of Tariff Reform, and resigned after 14 years' faithful representation. The next member was a young man, Mr. George Stewart Bowles, son of Gibson Bowles. He too struck on the rock of Tariff Reform. The committee of selection had apparently not ascertained his opinion but had taken it for granted that he was a Tariff Reformer, whereas he, like Sir Ernest Tritton was a Free Trader. Resignation followed, and Sir Harry Samuel succeeded him. Both Sir Harry and Lady Samuel were very popular but he was not a good platform speaker, and the local opposition delighted to heckle him until he became angry and lost the thread of his speech. The next member however, Sir Walter Greaves-Lord, could deal with all comers in debate, and was never beaten by either heckling or questioning. His elevation to the Bench in 1934 was the cause of Mr. Duncan Sandys becoming Norwood's member.

Among those who have contested the seat in the Liberal interest were Mr. P. W. Clayden, Dr. Verdon, Sir Alexander Lawrence, Mr. George Shrubsall, Mr. F. D. Lapthorn: in recent years the Labour party has gained in strength, and in 1934 Mrs. Barbara Ayrton Gould polled 12,799 votes. At the last electon Labour was successful, and Mr. Ronald Chamberlain was elected.

It is interesting to recall that the figures at the first election in 1885 were Bristowe 3,496, Clayden 2,563, the total being less than half the Labour poll in 1934. Mr. Duncan Sandys is a son-in-law of Mr. Winston Churchill, for he married Mr. Churchill's eldest daughter Diana in September 1935. Their marriage was heralded as a romance of the bye-election in Norwood when Mrs. Sandys' brother, Mr. Randolph Churchill, was the strongest supporter of Mr. Richard Findlay who opposed Mr. Sandys at that election.

In local Parliament the Progressives, as they were called, represented Norwood on the London County Council for some years. Messrs Hubbard and Shrubsall held the two seats and of late years in accordance with women coming to the front, Mrs. Dunn-Gardner, Mrs Worsthorne (until her marriage to Mr. Montague Norman, former Governor of the Bank of England), and Mrs. Gamble have sat with Capt. Marchant, O.B.E., as Municipal Reformers.

In the Guildhall Library is a report of a curious trial held in 1779. Humphrey Finnimore, reputed to be worth £40,000 was tried at the Town Hall, Southwark, on the charge of stealing five turkeys the property of Thomas Humphries who kept the "Sign of the Gipsies" at Norwood. The accused party also lived at Norwood and called as witnesses to his character, Catley, who kept the "Horns Tavern" and Dr. Allen, formerly Master of Dulwich College, and Mr. Allen, the contemporary Master. Finnimore was convicted by a jury, but the magistrates disagreed with the verdict, and on petition to the King the sentence was reversed.

Mr. Walford in his *Old and New London* Vol. VI. p. 316, writes:

"At Norwood, in 1833, died the Earl of Dudley, having been insane for the last few months of his life. He had always been eccentric; but in the early part of 1832 he was declared by Sir Henry Halford to be insane, having committed a variety of harmless extravagances."

Some years ago when an artesian well was sunk at the old brewery in Chapel Road some petrified oysters were found, and an abundance of marine fossils was also found during the excavation of the railway tunnel under Sydenham.

Although the district has changed so much, the

favourite Sunday evening walks round Norwood still remain to a certain extent unspoiled. True the favourite walk down Gibson's Hill and over the fields to Norbury Farm has gone, but it is still a pleasant walk from Gibson's Hill through the Grove and the Rookery, returning to Gibson's Hill via Streatham Common and the footpath to Arnulls Road. One can still take a pleasant walk through Gallery Road past the old Dulwich Picture Gallery and into Dulwich Park, which was often visited by Queen Mary when the rhododendrons were at their best: returning either via Union Road (now Hunt-slip Road) or continuing up through the old Dulwich toll-gate along College Road to the Crystal Palace. Or the walk from the Paxton Hotel through Kingswood Road, where Lord Vestey's estate, Kingswood House, is now being built upon, into College Road by Dulwich Wood, climbing the steep "Lovers Walk" into Sydenham Hill. West Norwood still has its points.

Index

In the index, a figure printed in italics indicates that there is *also* an illustration of the item indexed.